# VINEYARDS & WINERIES

# ACKNOWLEDGMENTS

We gratefully acknowledge the help of our representatives for their efficient and perceptive inspections of the lodging and dining establishments listed, the establishments' proprietors for their cooperation in showing their facilities and providing information about them, and the many users of previous editions who have taken the time to share their experiences. Mobil Travel Guide is also grateful to all the talented writers who contributed entries to this book.

Mobil, Exxon and Mobil Travel Guide are trademarks of Exxon Mobil Corporation or one of its subsidiaries. All rights reserved. Reproduction by any means, including, but not limited to, photography, electronic copying devices or electronic data processing, is prohibited. Use of information contained herein for solicitation of advertising or listing in any other publication is expressly prohibited without written permission from Exxon Mobil Corporation. Violations of reserved rights are subject to prosecution.

Copyright © 2008 Mobil Travel Guide. All rights reserved. This publication may not be reproduced in whole or in part by any means whatsoever without written permission from Mobil Travel Guide, 200 W. Madison St., Suite 3950, Chicago, IL 60606; info@mobiltravelguide.com.

Front cover images: Red Wine Corks: ©istockphoto.com/Valerie Loiseleux; Wine: ©istockphoto.com/Dušan Zidar; Perfect Wine Rack: ©istockphoto.com

All maps: ©Ken Gross for Rustbelt Cartography

The information contained herein is derived from a variety of third-party sources. Although every effort has been made to verify the information obtained from such sources, the publisher assumes no responsibility for inconsistencies or inaccuracies in the data or liability for any damages of any type arising from errors or omissions.

Neither the editors nor the publisher assume responsibility for the services provided by any business listed in this guide or for any loss, damage or disruption in your travel for any reason.

ISBN: 9-780841-60738-5          Manufactured in Canada.

10 9 8 7 6 5 4 3 2 1

# TABLE OF CONTENTS

POPULAR WINE REGIONS
| | |
|---|---|
| NAPA VALLEY | 12-39 |
| SONOMA VALLEY | 40-51 |
| CENTRAL COAST | 52-73 |
| OREGON WINE COUNTRY | 74-90 |
| WASHINGTON WINE COUNTRY | 91-105 |
| CANADA'S OKANAGAN VALLEY | 106-121 |

UNEXPECTED WINE REGIONS
| | |
|---|---|
| LONG ISLAND WINE COUNTRY | 123-133 |
| TEXAS HILL COUNTRY | 134-146 |
| VIRGINIA MONTICELLO WINE TRAIL | 147-161 |

| | |
|---|---|
| WINE UNFILTERED | 162-171 |
| INDEX & ART CREDITS | 172-176 |

# WRITTEN IN THE STARS

Because your time is precious and the travel world is ever-changing, having accurate travel information when you hit the road is essential. Mobil Travel Guide has provided the most trusted advice to travelers for more than 50 years.

The Mobil Corporation (known as Exxon Mobil Corporation since a 1999 merger) launched the Mobil Travel Guide books in 1958 following the introduction of the U.S. interstate highway system two years earlier. The first edition covered only five Southwestern states. Since then, our books have become the premier travel guides in North America, covering all 50 states and Canada. Recently, we've added international destinations, expanding the Mobil Travel Guide brand around the world.

Today, the concept of a "five star" experience is one that permeates the collective consciousness, but few people know that it's one that originated with Mobil. We created our star rating system to give travelers an easy to recognize quality scale for choosing where to stay and dine. Only Mobil's star ratings deliver a rigorously tested formula for determining if a hotel, restaurant or spa is as luxurious as its owners claim. Our rating system is the oldest in North America, and most hoteliers, restaurateurs and industry insiders understand the prestige and benefits that come with receiving a Mobil Star rating.

The Mobil Travel Guide process of rating each establishment includes unannouced inspections, incognito evaluations and a review of unsolicited comments from the general public.

We inspect more than 500 attributes at each property we visit, from cleanliness, to the condition of the rooms and public spaces, to employee attitude and courtesy. It's a system that rewards those properties that strive for and achieve excellence each year. And the very best properties raise the bar for those that wish to compete with them.

Only facilities that meet our standards earn the privilege of being listed in the guide. Properties are continuously updated, and deteriorating, poorly managed establishments are removed. We wouldn't recommend that you visit a hotel, restaurant or spa that we wouldn't want to visit ourselves.

If any aspect of your accommodation, dining, spa or sightseeing experience motivates you to comment, please contact us at Mobil Travel Guide, 200 W. Madison St., Suite 3950, Chicago, IL 60606, or send an email to info@mobiltravelguide.com. Happy travels.

# STAR RATINGS

## HOTELS

Whether you're looking for the ultimate in luxury or the best bang for your travel buck, we have a hotel recommendation for you. To help you pinpoint properties that meet your needs, Mobil Travel Guide classifies each lodging by type according to the following characteristics.

★★★★★The Mobil Five-Star hotel provides consistently superlative service in an exceptionally distinctive luxury environment. Attention to detail is evident throughout the hotel, resort or inn, from bed linens to staff uniforms.

★★★★The Mobil Four-Star hotel provides a luxury experience with expanded amenities in a distinctive environment. Services may include automatic turndown service, 24-hour room service and valet parking.

★★★The Mobil Three-Star hotel is well appointed, with a full-service restaurant and expanded amenities, such as a fitness center, golf course, tennis courts, 24-hour room service and optional turndown service.

★★The Mobil Two-Star hotel is considered a clean, comfortable and reliable establishment that has expanded amenities, such as a full-service restaurant.

★The Mobil One-Star lodging is a limited-service hotel, motel or inn that is considered a clean, comfortable and reliable establishment.

**Recommended** A Mobil-recommended property is a reliable, standout property new to our guides at press time that are simply listed in our pages. Look for a Mobil star-rating for these properties in the future.

For every property, we also provide pricing information. The pricing categories break down as follows:

$$ = Up to $150

$$ = $151-$250

$$$ = $251-$350

$$$$ = $351 and up

All prices quoted are accurate at the time of publication, however prices cannot be guaranteed.

QUAILS' GATE

## RESTAURANTS

All Mobil Star-rated dining establishments listed in this book have a full kitchen and most offer table service.

★★★★★The Mobil Five-Star restaurant offers one of few flawless dining experiences in the country. These establishments consistently provide their guests with exceptional food, superlative service, elegant décor and exquisite presentations of each detail surrounding a meal.

★★★★The Mobil Four-Star restaurant provides professional service, distinctive presentations and wonderful food.

★★★The Mobil Three-Star restaurant has good food, warm and skillful service and enjoyable décor.

★★The Mobil Two-Star restaurant serves fresh food in a clean setting with efficient service. Value is considered in this category, as is family friendliness.

★The Mobil One-Star restaurant provides a distinctive experience through culinary specialty, local flair or individual atmosphere.

Because menu prices can fluctuate, we list a pricing category rather than specific prices. The pricing categories are defined as follows, per diner, and assume that you order an appetizer or dessert, an entrée and one drink:

$= $15 and under

$$ = $16-$35

$$$ = $36-$85

$$$$ = $86 and up

## SPAS

Mobil Travel Guide's spa ratings are based on objective evaluations of more than 450 attributes. About half of these criteria assess basic expectations, such as staff courtesy, the technical proficiency and skill of the employees and whether the facility is clean and maintained properly. Several standards address issues that impact a guest's physical comfort and convenience, as well as the staff's ability to impart a sense of personalized service. Additional criteria measure the spa's ability to create a completely calming ambience.

★★★★★The Mobil Five-Star spa provides consistently superlative service in an exceptionally distinctive luxury environment with extensive amenities. The staff at a Mobil Five-Star spa provides extraordinary service beyond the traditional spa experience, allowing guests to achieve the highest level of relaxation and pampering. These spas offer an extensive array of treatments, often incorporating international themes and products. Attention to detail is evident throughout the spa, from arrival to departure.

★★★★The Mobil Four-Star spa provides a luxurious experience with expanded amenities in an elegant and serene environment. Throughout the spa facility, guests experience personalized service. Amenities might include, but are not limited to, single-sex relaxation rooms where guests wait for their treatments, plunge pools and whirlpools in both men's and women's locker rooms, and an array of treatments, including a selection of massages, body therapies, facials and a variety of salon services.

★★★The Mobil Three-Star spa is physically well appointed and has a full complement of staff.

# THE GOOD LIFE

Life doesn't get any sweeter than when you're traveling to wine country, where drinking and eating are revered. Good wine makes you smile, laugh, think, feel. From the moment you stick your nose in a round glass of cabernet and take your initial dizzying sip, sending tingles all the way down to your toes, you're drunk with pleasure. There's just something infectious about wine country: the people, the earthy-smelling tasting rooms, the idea of tasting wine you can't buy in a store. You may just want to drink it all in with great big gulps. But of course, you don't. You have many more tasting rooms to attend.

By the end of a day of wine tasting, your notes get smattered with wine (ours always do), your lips are purple, and you're starving. Since vineyards are essentially farms, they're usually located close enough to other agricultural ventures, whose delicious, earthy products—from cheese to vegetables to free-range meats—are served up at any one of the many charming, local bistros that dot the countryside. It's easy to find a romantic bistro at which you can settle in with yet another bottle of local wine and feast on just picked herb salads, steak frites or roasted vegetables while you plan the next day's adventures.

And then there are the deals. You'll end up shipping boxes of hard to find, reasonably priced wine home, no doubt. We had lots and lots of them waiting for us when we finished these tours. (Make sure you buy a wine refrigerator to stash your loot.) Every time you pull out a bottle at home, you'll remember your fabulous trip and share the stories about the incredible single-vineyard zinfandel you stumbled across in Napa or Sonoma.

So come along on this journey through wine country, from the East Coast to the West Cost and places in between. Contrary to what you may think, it's not all about Napa (although God bless that beautiful place). There are many other places in the U.S.A. that produce spectacular wines: California's Central Valley, Washington state (where you can find great wine in every quick mart), Oregon, Texas, Long Island. And then there's Canada, which has a beautiful wine country. We'll take you to the main regions, as well as the more unexpected ones. Our inspectors have stayed at all these hotels and dined in all these restaurants, which is actually very hard work (really!) to make sure your trip is luxurious from top to bottom.

Cheers,
The MTG crew

BERNARDUS LODGE AND WINERY

# POPULAR WINE
# REGIONS

DOMAINE SERENE

# CHAPTER 1
# NAPA VALLEY

*Carneros Inn ▪ Vintage Inn Garden ▪ Vintage Inn Guest Room ▪ Solage Calistoga*

It doesn't matter if you're a serious connoisseur or don't know the difference between a burgundy and a brut; both types of people populate Napa's tasting rooms to sniff, swirl and sip their way through this bucolic countryside, before retiring to one of the top-notch restaurants at night for even more wine and mouthwatering cuisine. That's Napa—and from a purely decadent point of view, it simply can't be beat.

With more than 200 wineries, Napa is one of the most famous wine regions in the world. You'll find all the major names in the biz here—Mondavi, Charles Krug, Beringer. There are the large estates (Rubicon) that look like they were transported from Italy, but there are also the smaller, less grand wineries that many visitors love to seek out, and that throw open their doors to guests. On the other hand, a few places keep them tightly shut, sealing in their "cult" status. It's a large, varied wine country (and not just in terms of soil), with much to see and taste.

Several small towns actually make up what everyone simply refers to as "Napa." The Napa Valley is about 30 miles long and includes the towns (from north to south) of Calistoga, St. Helena, Rutherford, Oakville, Yountville and Napa. Each has its particular charm. Calistoga has spas and hideaway hotels; St. Helena is full of shops; Yountville is something of a culinary mecca, lined with exceptional restaurants. Add to this the magnificent beauty of the place, and you'll want to make trip after trip to this wine capital.

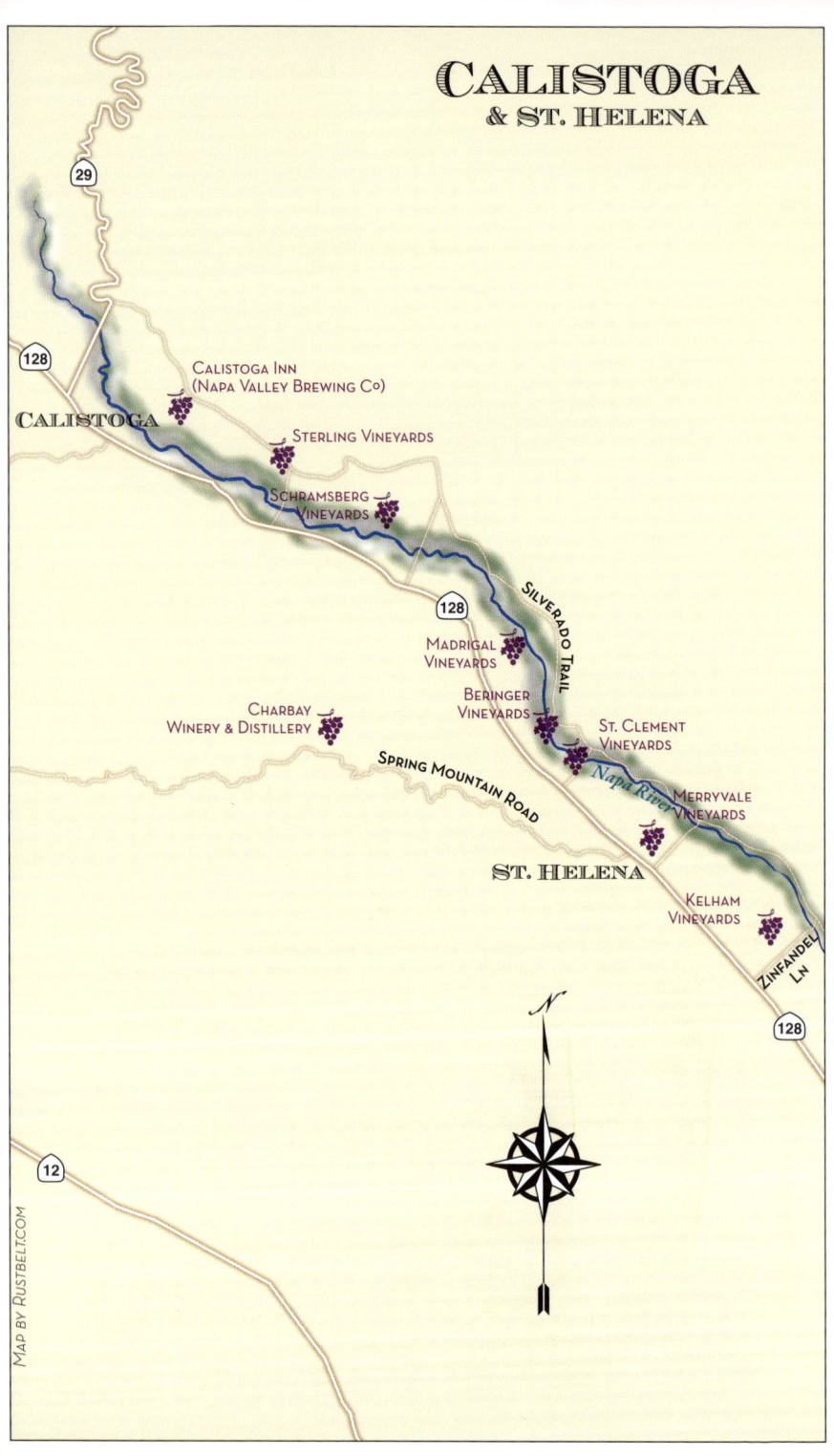

SOLAGE CALISTOGA

## CALISTOGA

Downtown Calistoga, with its quaint shops and restaurants, is a perfect place to spend an afternoon. Along with a plethora of wineries to visit, Calistoga's main strip, Lincoln Avenue, offers numerous art galleries and boutique storefronts. And though easy to overlook these days, more than 100 years ago, the volcanic mud and geothermal hot springs of Calistoga were the attractions that drew visitors to Napa Valley—not the wine. Most tourists head straight for Old Faithful, the other so-named gushing geyser that erupts as if on cue about every 30 minutes. Skip this tourist trap and instead appreciate the region's geological delights with a visit to a spa. Or simply sip your cares away at one of the town's reputed tasting rooms.

## TASTE

### Madrigal Vineyards
*3718 North St. Helena Highway, Calistoga, 707-942-6577; www.madrigalvineyards.com*
Since the 1930's, the Madrigal family has harvested grapes in the Napa Valley, and in 1995 they put that experience to good use, opening Madrigal Vineyards in the historic Larkmead District. If you're a fan of petite syrah, this is the place to pick up a bottle. The bold fruit flavor and rich, smooth finish keeps those in the know coming back year after year. Tour guides are friendly and the small-vineyard atmosphere is casual and welcoming; an ideal stop for wine country novices.
Monday-Friday 10 a.m.-3 p.m., by appointment.

### Calistoga Inn Restaurant and Brewery
*1250 Lincoln Ave., Calistoga, 707-942-4101; www.calistogainn.com*
Indulge your inner rebel and visit the first company to begin brewing beer commercially in Napa since Prohibition. With a full-time brewmaster, the facility creates award-winning beers and ales while limiting production to 450 barrels a year. Most of it is served on draft at the adjacent Calistoga Inn, where you'll find a restaurant, English-style pub and beer garden. On weekends hit the pub for rhythm-and-blues bands and come back Wednesdays

CALISTOGA RANCH

for open mic night. During the high season, live jazz guitar is played every night out on the patio.
Monday-Friday 11:30 a.m.-9:30 p.m., Saturday-Sunday 11:00 a.m.-10 p.m.

### Schramsberg Vineyards

*1400 Schramsberg Road, Calistoga, 707-942-4558; www.schramsberg.com*
Lauded as "America's first house of sparkling wine," Schramsberg is one of Napa's oldest vineyards and a mandatory stop for anyone who enjoys an occasional glass of bubbly. Guests are immediately wooed by the elaborate gardens surrounding the 19th-century home of the winery's founder, Jacob Schram. But the real treat comes on the tour, as enthusiastic guides take you through caves hand-dug by Chinese laborers in the late 19th century, revealing a collection of nearly two million bottles. The tour fee includes a sampling of three sparkling wines and one still variety (opt for the cabernet sauvignon if available), but be warned: after sipping on some of Schramsberg's special cuvées, you may never be able to enjoy a cheap bottle of sparkling again.
Tours: 10 a.m., 11:30 a.m., 12:30 p.m., 1:30 p.m. and 2:30 p.m. Reservations required. No children permitted.

### Sterling Vineyards

*1111 Dunaweal Lane, Calistoga, 707-942-3344, 800-726-6136; www.sterlingvineyards.com*
Take the aerial tramway up to Sterling Vineyards for the view and stay for the wine. In a whitewashed building modeled after villages on the Greek island of Mykonos, these vineyards helped establish chardonnay and merlot grapes in California. Take a self-guided tour of the premises and watch the winemaking operations from elevated walkways, sample current releases in the main tasting room or check out the Reserve Tasting and Cellar Club Rooms.
Daily 10:30 a.m.-4:30 p.m.

NAPA VALLEY

# STAY

### ★★★★Calistoga Ranch
*580 Lommel Road, Calistoga, 707-254-2800, 800-942-4220; www.calistogaranch.com*

This 46-room resort offers a quiet retreat after a day spent exploring local vineyards. Each room is housed in a free-standing lodge, decorated using natural materials with fireplaces, plush beds topped with down duvets and private outdoor showers. The onsite restaurant has a hearty American menu created by chef Eric Webster that is paired with local wines. A chef is also available to prepare a private dinner in guest lodges. The bathhouse spa features soaking pools and offers a full menu of luxurious treatments, such as wine body scrubs, while the fitness center, yoga deck and organized hikes will help you balance out all those calories you're blissfully consuming.
46 rooms. Restaurant. Fitness center. Spa. $$$$

*Calistoga Ranch • Schramsberg Vineyards • Solage Calistoga • Wappo Bar & Bistro*

### Solage Calistoga
*755 Silverado Trail, Calistoga, 866-942-7442; www.solagecalistoga.com*

As if the sprawling, scenic vineyards of Napa Valley aren't relaxing enough, Solage Calistoga brings eco-friendly luxury to the region with a brand new resort spanning 22 acres and boasting countless amenities, including complimentary cruiser bikes, daily movement classes, a mud bar and bathhouse, and geothermal spa pools. Modern, studio-style accommodations offer semi-private patios and flat-screen TVs, and the furnishings are all fashioned from reclaimed, natural products. Solage further embraces the green movement by implementing a recycling program and onsite composting. The restaurant, Solbar, uses locally grown produce from independent, organic farms to churn out such succulent dishes as lemon steamed local Petrale sole with Monterey artichokes and Sardinian couscous, and crispy veal sweetbreads with pea tendrils and house-cured maple bacon. After a stay here, you'll wonder why everyone doesn't go green.
89 rooms. Wireless Internet access. Restaurant, bar. Fitness center. Spa. Pool. $$$$

KULETO ESTATE WINERY

BERINGER VINEYARDS

## EAT

### ★★Wappo Bar & Bistro
*1226 Washington St., Calistoga, 707-942-4712; www.wappobar.com*
A charming bistro located in a small, yellow house with a beautiful tree-lined courtyard, this restaurant offers small and large plates that run the culinary gamut. Nibble on everything from Thai coconut curry with prawns and vegetables to Tandoori chicken with lemon basmati rice. In warmer weather, snag a seat on the charming outdoor patio. International menu. Lunch, dinner. Closed Tuesday. $$

## SPA

### ★★★★The Bathhouse
*580 Lommel Road, Calistoga, 707-254-2820; www.calistogaranch.com*
The Bathhouse at Calistoga Ranch was opened in 2004 by the group behind sister property Auberge du Soleil and features five treatment rooms, inspired by the native landscape and designed with organic elements such as copper, stone, wood and water. Three of the treatment rooms feature large terraces with soaking tubs and showers, and all are tailor-made for treatments involving a bath: buttermilk baths, mud baths or thermal mineral pool soaks. The spa draws water from the local hot springs and uses Napa Valley ingredients, including honey, grapeseed and bay laurel, in many of the treatments. The mud wrap promises to boost immunity. Morning yoga takes place in the resort's wine cave.

## SHOP

### Ca'toga Galleria d'Arte
*1206 Cedar St. (just off Lincoln Ave.), Calistoga, 707-942-3900; www.catoga.com*
See the works of Italian muralist Carlo Marchiori, which include ceramics, tiles, paintings, sculptures and furniture in Neo-Classical and Baroque styles. Thursday-Monday.

### Hurd Beeswax Candles
*1255 Lincoln Ave., Calistoga, 707-942-7410; www.hurdbeeswaxcandles.com*
This charming shop offers demonstrations of candle-making from pure beeswax. Watch the artisans create their wares and then pick up some brightly

colored, all-natural sticks to take home. Sunday-Thursday 10 a.m.-5:30 p.m., Friday-Saturday 10 a.m.-8 p.m.

**Main Element**
*1333A Lincoln Ave., Calistoga, 707-942-6347*
A welcoming space in downtown Calistoga, this gallery exhibits upscale, locally made wine country art and furnishings. Wares include everything from colorful, hand-blown stemware to handcrafted wood rocking chairs.
10 a.m.-6 p.m.

## ST. HELENA

About eight miles southeast of Calistoga, St. Helena reigns supreme among wine country-bound connoisseurs. It is home to just more than 6,000 residents and because it sits between the reflecting slopes of the Mayacamas and Vaca mountains, it enjoys hotter temperatures than other areas of Napa Valley. An ideal base for wide-ranging exploration, the city is home to the **Culinary Institute of America at Greystone** (*2555 Main St., St. Helena, 707-967-1010; www.ciachef.edu*), where you can watch cooking demonstrations and dine on the terrace at the school's Greystone restaurant. As you're driving through St. Helena, CA-29 turns into Main Street, St. Helena's main historic downtown thoroughfare. Here you'll find plenty of shops for browsing—and picking up snacks before hitting the wineries.

## TASTE

**Beringer Vineyards**
*2000 Main St., St. Helena, 707-967-4412; www.beringer.com*
Beringer has welcomed guests since 1934, making it the oldest continuously operating winery in the Napa Valley. Sign up for one of the comprehensive tours, which include a walk through hand-dug, aging tunnels as well as informative talks about how wine is made and aged—followed, of course, by wine tasting. 10 a.m.-6 p.m., May 30-October 23, 10 a.m.-5 p.m., October 24-May 29.

**Charbay Winery & Distillery**
*4001 Spring Mountain Road, St. Helena, 707-963-9327; www.charbay.com*
Although wine is only a small percent of the focus here, the result is no less impressive. Infused flavored vodkas, from original and green tea to pomegranate and ruby red grapefruit, along with other spirits including whiskey, rum and pastis, keep this family-run property busy year-round. The worthwhile one-hour tour outlines the basics of distillation and gives you a chance to sample Charbay's prized Oakville Cabernet Sauvignon—unfortunately, the law prohibits tastings of their distilled spirits.
Saturday, by appointment only.

**Kelham Vineyards**
*360 Zinfandel Lane, St. Helena, 707-963-2000; www.kelhamvineyards.com*
A true family affair, the Kelhams have been farming on their 60-acre vineyard for more than 35 years. Before producing its own label, the vineyard harvested its premium grapes for such esteemed vintners as Cakebread, Mondavi and Beaulieu. Unlike some of the larger estates in the area, Kelham's offers only formal wine tastings, a seated affair either in the tasting room or out on the veranda, where vineyard owner and host Susanna Kelham explains the intimate process behind each of the wines presented.
By appointment only.

BERINGER VINEYARDS RHINE HOUSE

### Kuleto Estate Vineyard

*2470 Sage Canyon Road, St. Helena, 707-963-9750; www.kuletoestate.com*
Spanning 761 acres of wild hillside land on the eastern edge of Napa Valley, this family estate blends unique architecture—think Frank Lloyd Wright meets a Tuscan villa—with award-winning wines and expansive natural surroundings overlooking Lake Hennessey. Originally a designer and restaurateur, the vineyard's founder, Pat Kuleto, carried his love of food and wine directly to the soil, harvesting hillside-grown grapes for more than a decade and yielding wines full of richness and depth. The intimate tour includes four wines and complimentary food pairings ($35 per person). Afterward, relax on the rustic patio to savor your wine and the gorgeous setting. One sip of Kuleto's Tuscan-style sangiovese, and you'll be hard-pressed to leave without a case.
Tours: Monday-Saturday 10:30 a.m. and 2:30 p.m., Sunday 10:30 a.m. and 1 p.m. Reservations required.

### Merryvale Vineyards

*1000 Main St., St. Helena, 707-963-7777; www.merryvale.com*
Specializing in wine education, this winery offers a variety of programs for both the experienced connoisseur and the novice. The popular Saturday and Sunday 10:30 a.m. Wine Component Tasting seminars include a tour of the historic winery with its spectacular cask room. With 2,000-gallon oak casks on display, the cask room is regarded as one of the most enchanting places to drink wine in Napa Valley. Merryvale produces distinct chardonnays as well as bordeaux-blend red wine.
Daily 10 a.m.-6:30 p.m.

### St. Clement Vineyards

*2867 St. Helena Highway, St. Helena, 800-331-8266; www.stclement.com*
Originally built in 1878 by a San Francisco manufacturer of fine mirror and glass, the Rosenbaum House is the focal point of St. Clement, offering peerless views from the front porch's café and an intimate tasting room inside. The tour elaborates upon the history of the Victorian mansion and the surrounding winery, though much of the fruit used to produce St. Clem-

NAPA VALLEY

ent's wine is purchased from other vineyards. Cabernet sauvignon, chardonnay, sauvignon blanc and merlot are made at this boutique winery, but the shining star is the Oroppas, a meritage-style blend of full-bodied excellence.

Daily 10 a.m.–5 p.m. Reservations recommended.

## STAY

### ★★★The Inn at Southbridge
*1020 Main St., St. Helena,*
*707-967-9400, 800-520-6800;*
*www.innatsouthbridge.com*

Renowned architect William Turnbull Jr. had the small-town squares of Italy in mind when he designed this upscale, contemporary inn. Soft cream stucco buildings house spacious guest quarters with vaulted ceilings, fireplaces and French doors opening onto private balconies with views of the courtyard. Amenities include terrycloth bathrobes, down comforters and Gilchrist & Soames bathroom products. The scenic property also includes Merryvale Winery, Tra Vigne restaurant and Pizzeria Tra Vigne.

21 rooms. Complimentary continental breakfast. High-speed Internet access. Restaurant, bar. Spa. $$$$

### ★★★★Meadowood Napa Valley
*900 Meadowood Lane, St. Helena,*
*707-963-3646, 800-458-8080;*
*www.meadowood.com*

Spanning 250 wine-country acres, Meadowood is large, but its staff is attentive—from the esteemed resident wine tutor to the guest services manager assigned to each arriving visitor. The owners also run **Screaming Eagle Vineyards** (*7557 Silverado Trail, Napa, 707-944-0749; www.screamingeagle.com*) which has a product so exclusive you have to join a mailing list to get a bottle. Enjoy a game of croquet, tennis or golf, or simply lounge by the pool. The suites, cottages and lodges blend classic country style and California sensibilities with their stone fireplaces, skylights, vaulted ceilings, private decks and luxurious bathrooms—not to mention plenty of modern amenities such as flat-screen TVs, DVD/CD players, coffee and tea pots and toasters. The Grill is available for casual dining under the shade of an umbrella, and the restaurant turns out eager-to-please gastronomic delights.

85 rooms. Wireless Internet access. Two restaurants, three bars. Children's activity center. Fitness center. Spa. Pool. $$$$

## EAT

### ★★★Martini House
*1245 Spring St., St. Helena,*
*707-963-2233; www.martinihouse.com*

The cuisine at this 1923 Craftsman-style bungalow is fresh and flavorful, but for many the extensive drink list is reason enough to show up. The restaurant has a 600-bottle wine list, many specialty cocktails and a large beer selection. The ambiance is no less impressive—renowned restaurant designer Pat Kuleto's eye for style incorporates Napa Valley's Native American history with deep burgundy leather booths and several fireplaces. (Be sure to visit his winery; *see pg. 20*.) The earthy ingredients weaved throughout the menu complement the restaurant's casual upscale appeal and keeps guests satisfied with dishes such as butter-basted Alaskan halibut with curry-toasted almond crust and golden raisins. The outdoor garden, surrounded by vine-covered arbors and an antique fountain, is an ideal spot for dining on a temperate evening.

California menu. Lunch, dinner.

GUESTROOM BALCONY AT MEADOWOOD

Closed two weeks in January. Bar. Business casual attire. Reservations recommended. Outdoor seating. $$$

### ★★★The Restaurant Bar & Terrace
*900 Meadowood Lane, St. Helena, 707-967-1205; www.meadowood.com/winecuisine/the-restaurant*
Remaining true to Meadowood's natural, serene setting, The Restaurant concentrates on the purity of regional flavors, using several ingredients from the resort's onsite garden. The result is a menu replete with fresh, delectable choices, including organic strawberries and foie gras with aged Balsamic and garden arugula, and roasted turbot with artichoke, caper-berry and preserved lemon. From the extensive list of 950 wines, sommelier Rom Toulon assists in pairing varietals to fully complement the essence of each dish. There are numerous prix fixe and à la carte options, but those in the know leave their evening in the hands of executive chef Christopher Kostow, whose nightly tasting menu epitomizes the casual elegance of California's wine country. A modern dining room with stone fireplaces, white wainscoting and rows of windows revealing the beautiful grounds adds to the dreamlike experience.
California menu. Dinner. Closed Sunday. Bar. Children's menu. Jackets recommended. Reservations recommended. Outdoor seating. $$$$

### ★★★★Terra
*1345 Railroad Ave., St. Helena, 707-963-8931; www.terrarestaurant.com*
Chef and owner Hiro Sone has been wowing diners at Terra, his cozy, intimate Napa Valley restaurant, since 1988. Set one block off the main drag on Railroad Avenue in St. Helena, Terra is located in a charming, old stone building, rustically finished with vintage red-tiled floors, exposed stone walls and wood-beamed ceilings. The food is spectacular—a successful blend of flavors from Italy, France and Asia. Signature dishes change with the seasons and include grilled free range veal chop with forest mushrooms, grilled Hokkaido scallops, and chocolate truffle cake with espresso ice cream and fudge sauce. With gracious hospitality and warmth, the staff at Terra makes you feel like you're dining at home.
French menu, Italian menu. Dinner. Closed Tuesday and two weeks in early January. Business casual attire. Reservations recommended. $$$

# NAPA VALLEY

## Dean & Deluca
*607 South St. Helena Highway, St. Helena, 707-967-9980; www.deandeluca.com*
You don't have to visit New York to enjoy this gourmet grocer's quality foods, not to mention its respect for regional tastes. Along with products from around the world, the shop showcases fresh, local ingredients and area specialties, most dramatically in its prepared food section. You'll also find local produce, artisanal cheeses, 1,400 kinds of California wine, an espresso bar and lots more. All of which make it the perfect place to pick up goods for a picnic.
Monday-Friday 9 a.m.-7 p.m., Saturday-Sunday 9 a.m.-8 p.m. The espresso bar is open Sunday-Thursday 7 a.m.-7 p.m., Friday-Saturday 7 a.m.-8 p.m.

## The Model Bakery
*1357 Main St., St. Helena, 707-963-8192; www.themodelbakery.com*
This bakery is a St. Helena institution, with an 80-plus year history. Don't miss the signature pain du vin, cheese baguettes (we couldn't get enough

Dining at Meadowood Napa Valley • St. Clement Winery • Kuleto Estate Vineyard • Martini House

of these) and walnut bread. They also make creamy soups and hearty brick-oven baked pizza. Needless to say, the shop is a great place to pick up a picnic lunch.
Tuesday-Saturday 7 a.m.-6 p.m., Sunday 7 a.m.-4 p.m.; winter hours are Tuesday-Saturday 7 a.m.-5:30 p.m., Sunday 7 a.m.-4 p.m.

## Taylor's Automatic Refresher
*933 Main St., St. Helena, 707-963-3486; www.taylorsrefresher.com*
If you can't imagine a greasy patty melt and a smooth glass of pinot noir going together, you haven't been to Taylor's. This old-school roadside burger shack, ownod by winemaker Joel Gott, has developed a cult following with visitors and locals alike. And for good reason: The burgers are tasty and generous and the signature garlic fries, tossed in garlic butter and parsley are positively addicting (and make the often lengthy wait in line worth it). Try to avoid the lunch rush to guarantee a seat at one of the shaded picnic tables. The concept has been so successful there are now sister restaurants in Napa and San Francisco.
Diner menu. Lunch, dinner. Closed holidays. Casual attire. Outdoor seating. $

NAPA SOAP COMPANY

AUBERGE DU SOLEIL

## SPA

### ★★★★The Spa at Meadowood
*900 Meadowood Lane, St. Helena, 800-458-8080;*
*www.meadowood.com/wellness*

Massages delivered fireside, a rejuvenating facial with organic ingredients, a relaxing yoga class. These are just some of the pampering, incredibly indulgent services available at this wine country spa. Signature treatments include the Meadowood Harvest Wrap, which begins with a hot towel compress that prepares your skin for a tea tree exfoliant and ends with your body swaddled in warm towels and blankets while you soak in the benefits of a hydrating body masque. If you're short on time, opt for the 30-minute foot relief, which includes just enough pressure-point relieving massage to invigorate you for another day of wine tasting.

## SHOP

### Napa Soap Company
*651 Main St., St. Helena, 707-963-5010;*
*www.napasoapcompany.com*

Find all-natural soaps made from local Napa Valley ingredients like grapeseed oil, lavender, herbs, beeswax, honey and even a little cabernet. The shop is located just south of downtown.
Daily 10 a.m.-5 p.m.

### Olivier Napa Valley
*1375 Main St., St. Helena, 707-967-8777;*
*www.oliviernapavalley.com*

Pop in this storefront right on St. Helena's main drag and indulge in its vast selection of gourmet olive oils, sauces and other savory items. Whether you're in the market for one of nearly a dozen flavored oils or just curious to taste caramelized shallot dark beer mustard (which, by the way, is delicious), Olivier's will have your taste buds buzzing within minutes of stepping inside.
Monday-Saturday 10 a.m.-6 p.m., Sunday 10 a.m.-5 p.m.

### Woodhouse Chocolate
*1367 Main St., St. Helena, 800-966-3468,*
*707-963-8413;*
*www.woodhousechocolate.com*

This cozy, butter-yellow colored shop sells handcrafted chocolates, truffles and toffees. The business is a family affair, started by a couple that left

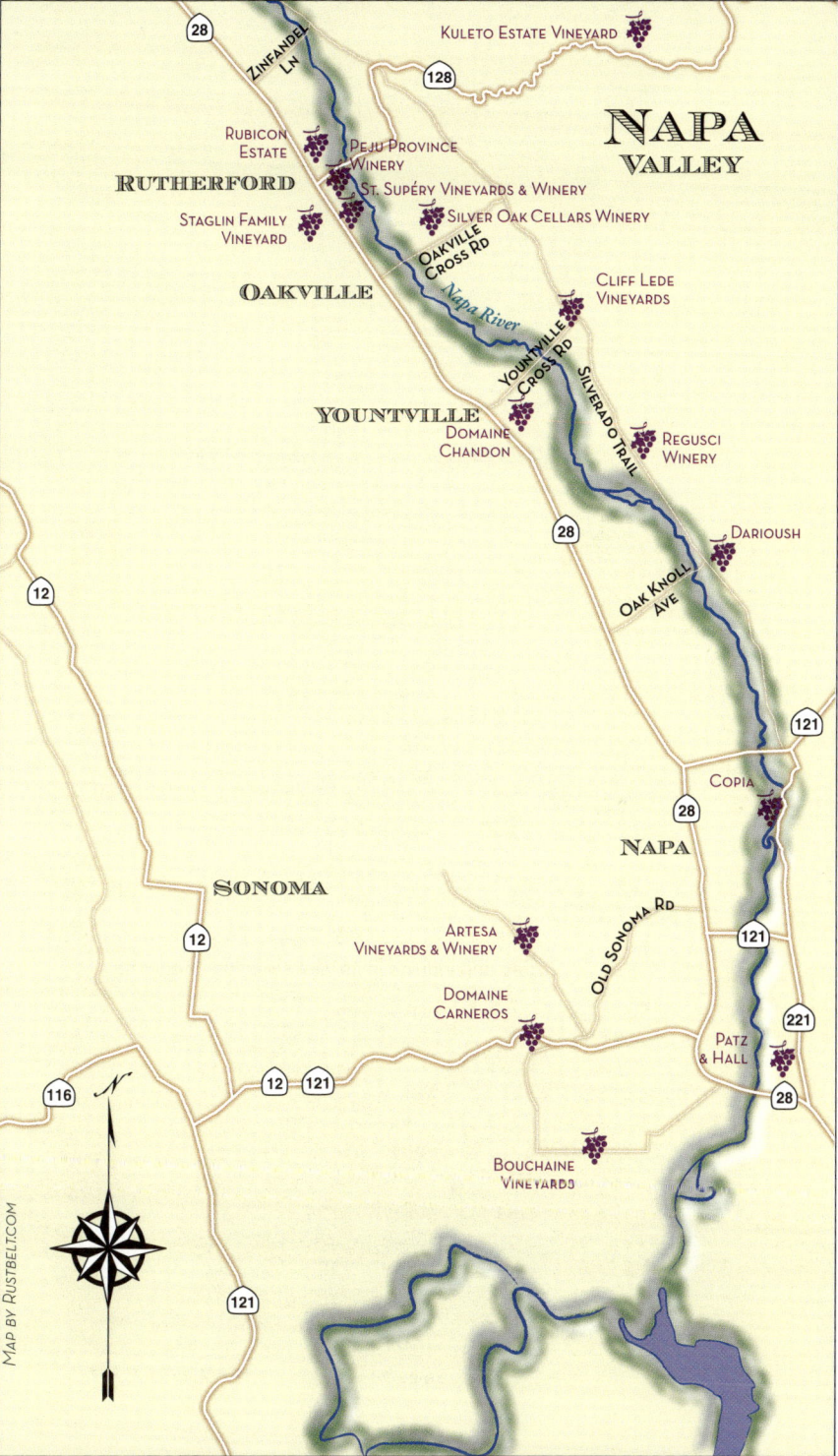

PEJU PROVINCE WINERY

the wine business for the upscale chocolate trade, an effort that has been a sweet success.
Daily 10:30 a.m.-5:30 p.m.

## RUTHERFORD

A little more than four miles south of St. Helena on CA-29 is the small hamlet of Rutherford, home to one of the top hotels in Napa Valley. While there are plenty of wineries to visit here, one of the best reasons to stop off in Rutherford is another kind of tasting—olive oil, at **Round Pond Olive Mill** (see box at left). But first things first—wine. Rutherford's dry, loamy soil and nearly year-round sunshine provide an ideal environment for growing cabernet grapes, which explains why cabernet sauvignon reigns supreme here, and why some of Napa Valley's biggest wineries call Rutherford home.

## TASTE

### Peju Province Winery
*8466 St. Helena Highway, Rutherford, 707-963-3600; www.peju.com*
Though many come for the wine, they often stay for the entertainment. This exquisite estate, replete with a unique castle-like copper-topped tower, a reflecting pool, fountains and beautifully landscaped gardens, appeals to all the senses with tastings, cooking classes, art exhibits and more. The wines aren't too shabby, either. In fact, Peju's Reserve 2004 Cabernet Sauvignon is one of the best in the region.
Daily 10 a.m.-6 p.m.

### Rubicon Estate
*1991 St. Helena Highway, Rutherford, 707-968-1161; www.rubiconestate.com*
If you take one winery tour while visiting Napa, make it Rubicon. The knowledgeable and engaging tour guides will fill you in on how Francis Ford Coppola came to own this winery, and how he brought it full circle. It's the kind of story that makes movie magic, but this vineyard has no Hollywood flash. While you can easily envision Coppola sitting at one of the outside tables puffing on a stogie, the vineyard, which looks like it was transported from Italy, is where the famous director quietly raised his family

NAPA VALLEY

> ## ANOTHER KIND OF TASTING
> Grapes are not the only little round fruits that thrive in this region. **Round Pond Olive Mill** (*888-302-2575; www.roundpond.com*) produces some of the valley's finest gourmet olive oils. You could easily spend an entire afternoon here. For the full experience, make reservations for the alfresco lunch, tour the olive mill and learn about the meticulous cold-press process behind Round Pond's four signature oils: Italian varietal, Spanish varietal, blood orange and Meyer lemon. A guide will lead you through tastings of each paired with vinegars (also made here), fresh organic produce and gourmet bread. The afternoon is topped off with a family-style lunch of local cheeses, meats, fruits and olive oil cake for dessert. On the third Saturday of every month from noon-4 p.m., purchase fresh olive oil straight from the spigot. They also make wine at the charming vineyard across the street.
>
> Olive oil tastings are by appointment only. Wine tastings are offered daily from 11 a.m.-4 p.m. by appointment.

outside of the spotlight, and where he and his wife still reside. You may also be surprised by how good the wines are, particularly the Rutherford Edizione Pennino Zinfandel (the label has a picture of Italy and the Statue of Liberty, a homage to Francis' grandfather) and the Rutherford Cabernet Sauvignon, a tribute to the stylized cabernets of the previous owner.
Daily 10 a.m.-5 p.m.

### St. Supéry Vineyards and Winery
*8440 St. Helena Highway, Rutherford, 707-963-4507; www.stsupery.com*
This center provides a hands-on lesson in grape-growing and winemaking, from planting through bottling. Its "SmellaVision" course enables you to deconstruct a wine's bouquet. You can take a free self-guided tour or sign up for a one-hour guided tour, held daily at 1 p.m. and 3 p.m., as well as participate in tastings and sampling the small production wines in the reserve tasting library.
Daily 10 a.m.-5 p.m.

### Staglin Family Vineyard
*1570 Bella Oaks Lane, Rutherford, 707-944-0477; www.staglinfamily.com*
Located behind its more famous neighbor, Robert Mondavi Vineyards, Staglin Family is a true family-run, locally-loved vineyard. This by-appointment-only winery produces some of the area's most highly regarded cabernet sauvignon in the valley. The tour ends in the underground wine caves, as you're invited to pull up a chair at the grand dining room table and taste the fruits of their labor—literally.
Monday-Friday 11 a.m.-3 p.m.; reservations required.

PEJU PROVINCE WINERY

# STAY

### ★★★Auberge du Soleil
*180 Rutherford Hill Road, Rutherford, 707-963-1211, 800-348-5406; www.aubergedusoleil.com*

This sun-drenched sanctuary is perched on a quiet, 33-acre hillside olive grove in Rutherford. What once began as simply a Provence-inspired restaurant in 1981 is now a full-fledged sanctuary. Luxurious touches include Italian linens, plasma TVs, wet bars with stocked refrigerators (full-sized in suites), espresso machines, large soaking tubs, CD players with a choice of CDs, wine, daily fresh fruit and a personal welcome note. Be sure to visit the exclusive spa featuring Meyer lemon olive oil massages, among other treats, and the indulgent private Melisse Suite. The accommodations portion of the resort was recently gated to ensure maximum privacy.
52 rooms. Wireless Internet access. Children over 16 only. Restaurant, bar. Fitness center. Spa. Pool. Tennis. Business center. $$$$

# EAT

### ★★★★Auberge du Soleil Restaurant
*180 Rutherford Hill Road, Rutherford, 707-963-1211, 800-348-5406; www.aubergedusoleil.com*

French-born San Francisco restaurateur Claude Rouas set out to create a Provence-like destination restaurant in northern California when he opened Auberge du Soleil in 1981. Diners liked it so much they demanded overnight accommodations—and received them four years later. The seasonal French-California menu features artisanal ingredients and products from local farms, spotlighted in dishes such as English pea risotto with wild shrimp and applewood smoked bacon, Delta asparagus soup with shitake mushrooms, and roasted lamb with gnocchi. Don't miss the local cheese selections for dessert. The six-course tasting menu is available with wines to match from the large, locally strong list. If you're touring the valley by car, consider a lunch stop where you can enjoy the views from the terrace.
California, French menu. Breakfast, lunch, dinner. Bar. Business casual attire. Reservations required. Valet parking. Outdoor seating. $$$$

NAPA VALLEY

## SPA

### ★★★★The Auberge du Soleil Spa
*180 Rutherford Hill Road, Rutherford, 707-963-1211, 866-228-2490; www.aubergedusoleil.com*

The glorious Napa Valley surroundings have inspired this spa's philosophy, with vineyard, garden and valley themes dominating the treatment menu. Nutrient-rich grapeseed and locally grown herbs and flowers are the foundation for the vineyard's massages, body treatments and facials. Seasonal treatments are also a highlight of a visit to this spa, where a couple's bath with grapefruit and juniper is featured in spring, a luscious peaches-and-cream body mask in summer, a harvest-inspired cleanse in fall, and a peppermint-and-eucalyptus body treatment in winter.

## YOUNTVILLE

There is no better place for true gourmet sustenance than Yountville—at least in wine country. In fact, it's often referred to as the "culinary capital of the Napa

*Cliff Lede Vineyards • Peju Province Winery • Auberge du Soleil • Auberge du Soleil Restaurant*

Valley" and with good reason. There is a slew of fine restaurants here to keep your wine-tasting well balanced. When you're not feasting, take a stroll down Washington Street (the main strip), where you'll find inviting inns and quaint boutique shops.

## TASTE

### Cliff Lede Vineyards
*1473 Yountville Cross Road, Yountville, 707-944-8642; www.cliffledevineyards.com*

Claiming 60 acres of Napa Valley's Stags Leap District, the Cliff Lede Vineyards utilize state-of-the-art techniques, including gravity-flow and berry-by-berry sorting systems to produce some of the best cabernet sauvignon in the region, along with sauvignon blanc and claret varietals. Tours of the vineyard, which commence in the perfectly restored craftsman-style tasting room, are small and informative, but the real treat is relaxing on one of the cozy porch swings, which offers views of the Lede vineyards and beyond. Another great post-tasting option is to stroll through the property's art gallery.
Daily 10 a.m.-5 p.m.; private tours by appointment.

VINTAGE INN

THE FRENCH LAUNDRY

### Domaine Chandon
*1 California Drive, Yountville, 707-944-2280;*
*www.chandon.com*
Founded in 1973 by the parent company of Champagne maker Moët & Chandon, Domaine Chandon is one of the leading sparkling wine producers in the United States. You'll feel the true romance of the place when you tour the winery and the beautifully landscaped premises. On the terrace adjacent to the tasting salon, you can sip some bubbly and enjoy lunch outdoors, a fitting conclusion to a jaunt into wine country.
May-October, Monday-Thursday 10 a.m.-6 p.m., Friday-Sunday 10 a.m.-7 p.m., November-April, daily 10 a.m.-6 p.m.

## STAY

### ★★★Vintage Inn
*6541 Washington St., Yountville, 707-944-1112, 800-351-1133; www.vintageinn.com*
Inspired by the country inns of France, this intimate property sits on three-and-a-half acres of beautifully lush surroundings in the heart of wine country. After a day of vineyard hopping, relax in bright, spacious rooms with private patios or balconies, wood-beamed ceilings and large fireplaces, or lounge by the heated outdoor pool. The daily champagne breakfast buffet is a local favorite and if you're still hungry, there's afternoon tea or coffee and cookies.
80 rooms. Wireless Internet access. Complimentary full breakfast. Two restaurants. Bar. Pool. $$$

## EAT

### ★★★Bouchon
*6534 Washington St., Yountville, 707-944-8037;*
*www.bouchonbistro.com*
If you can't get into The French Laundry, try Thomas Keller's more casual French bistro. Like most Napa Valley restaurants, the fare is seasonal, but Bouchon maintains a decidedly bistro flavor, right down to the pommes frites, chalkboard specials and newspaper rack by the nickel bar. You can't go wrong with any of the fresh seafood, and the comfort dishes like slow-braised pork short ribs and croque madame are especially enjoyable. Desserts include pot de crème and profiteroles with vanilla ice cream and chocolate sauce. Be sure to

stop by the next-door Bouchon Bakery. The éclairs and macarons are spectacular.

French menu. Lunch, dinner, late-night. Bar. Business casual attire. Reservations recommended. Outdoor seating. $$$

### ★★★★★The French Laundry
*6640 Washington St., Yountville, 707-944-2380; www.frenchlaundry.com*
At this former French steam laundry, chef Thomas Keller has raised the standard for fine dining in America. While the country locale—a circa-1900 rock and timber cottage—makes diners feel at home, tables topped with limoges china, crystal stemware and floor-length linens, set the tone for the nine-course French or vegetarian tasting menus that change daily but always rely on seasonal produce and organic meats. Dishes are small and prompt contemplation on the perfect marriage of fresh, pristine ingredients on each plate. The affable staff keeps the experience casual and comfortable, yet refined and memorable. Reservations are taken two months in advance, so be prepared if you're hoping to snag a table at this perennially outstanding American classic.
French menu. Lunch (Friday-Sunday), dinner. Closed two weeks in January and one week in late July-early August. Reservations required. Jackets required for lunch and dinner. $$$$

### ★★★Redd
*6480 Washington St., Yountville, 707-944-2222; www.reddnapavalley.com*
Locals love to love Redd, Napa's newest epicurean destination. This chic restaurant represents chef/owner Richard Reddington's view of wine country cuisine with influences from all over the map. The unadorned white-walled interior and wood doorframe speak to the simplicity of Reddington's cooking. But don't think you're getting bland basics here. You'll be won over by such dishes as Alaskan halibut with chickpea purée, sweet peppers, prosciutto and salt cod beignets, and organic chicken with faro, bacon and asparagus saltimbocca. For dessert, the red wine tart with spring fruits and fontainebleu is a perfect complement to any of the varietals on the wine list.
Contemporary American menu. Lunch, dinner, Sunday brunch. Bar. Business casual attire. Reservations recommended. Outdoor seating. $$$

## NAPA

After so much quaintness, the city of Napa can seem overly urban at first glance. Interestingly, the town was named for the valley, not the other way around. But even Napa has its charms. Take Yountville Cross Road over to Silverado Trail to escape the traffic and get a better glimpse of the rolling hills and expansive vineyards. The best place to start is probably COPIA—Napa Valley's equivalent of a cultural museum.

## TASTE

### Artesa Vineyard & Winery
*1345 Henry Road, Napa, 707-224-1668; www.artesawinery.com*
A striking contrast to the restored historic vineyards so common to Napa Valley, the region's newest winery has sleek, modernist architecture and its own artist in residence. Built by the Codorniu family,

THE CARNEROS INN

Spain's largest makers of sparkling wine, Artesa (which means craftsman and suggests that something is handcrafted in the Catalan language) started with sparkling but has since expanded to quality still wines.
Daily 10 a.m.-5 p.m.

### Bouchaine Vineyards
*1075 Buchli Station Road, Napa, 800-654-9463; www.bouchaine.com*
Boasting 85 acres, Bouchaine is best known for its pinot noir, a grape that thrives in the cool Carneros region. Renovated extensively in 1995, the winery received numerous local architectural and historic awards, due in part to its use of recycled materials. The end result is a fireplace-warmed tasting room, as well as a deck and terrace with hill views, which make for cozy wine tastings.
Daily 10:30 a.m.-4 p.m.

### COPIA
*500 First St., Napa, 707-259-1600, 888-512-6742; www.copia.org*
Billing itself as "America's center for wine, food, and the arts," and appropriately named after the Roman goddess of abundance, COPIA has much to offer. You're free to mill about the two sleekly designed floors. On the ground floor, you'll be offered a free tasting of wine the minute you walk in. To the right, the COPIA Store gift shop has a huge selection of cookbooks, Riedel wine glasses, COPIA cookware, and wine and table accessories. Each day the center boasts a full schedule of lectures, cooking demonstrations and exhibits. The in-house theater is a great place to spend an evening enjoying dinner and a movie. Dinner can be had in **Julia's Kitchen**, a restaurant inspired by none other than Julia Child. (You can see an installation of her cookware just outside.) Julia's serves French-California cuisine featuring the fresh produce from COPIA's edible gardens.
Daily 10 a.m.-6 p.m.

## Darioush

*4240 Silverado Trail, Napa, 707-257-2345; www.darioush.com*

A visit to Darioush is more akin to a journey to ancient Persia than Napa Valley. From the 16 monumental freestanding columns greeting visitors as they enter to the richly textured travertine stone surrounding the entire compound to the amphitheater used for special events and performances, Darioush vineyard is an experience in itself. Proprietor Darioush Khaledi grew up in Iran's shiraz region, bringing his international expertise to California's famous wine country in 1997. The results are award-winning. The chardonnays, viogniers and cabernet sauvignons are all smooth and well balanced, and the signature shiraz is not to be missed. The large tasting bar resembles something of an extravagant hafla (an Arabic dance party)—it can get packed and quite lively.

Daily 10:30 a.m.-5 p.m.

## Domaine Carneros

*1240 Duhig Road, Napa, 800-716-2788; www.domainecarneros.com*

Those looking to embrace the essence of France without flying across the Atlantic need go no further than Domaine Carneros. The property occupies prime real estate in the heart of Napa and its apex, the majestic Domaine Carneros chateau, was modeled after an historic 18th-century mansion owned by the Taittinger family near Epernay, France. The winery specializes in sparkling wines including brut, brut rose and blanc de blancs, and uses only locally grown grapes to gain the perfect delicate balance of flavors. In lieu of a traditional tasting, Domaine offers flights, as well as full glass or bottle table service in the main chateau or along the back terrace. Caviar and other savory hors d'oeuvres are also available, set to match the bottles of bubbly. Though not the cheapest option, it certainly costs a lot less than a flight to Paris.

Daily 11 a.m., 1 p.m. and 3 p.m.

## Patz & Hall

*851 Napa Valley Corporate Way, Suite A, Napa, 707-265-7700; www.patzhall.com*

Since 2006, Patz and Hall has taken the concept of wine tasting a step further, creating a comfortable offsite salon to enjoy its single-vineyard varietals. Boasting a living room-like atmosphere with artwork on the walls and plush seating arrangements, the Patz & Hall Tasting Salon affords passionate wine aficionados and curious newbies the opportunity to sample, converse and compare different wines in a laid-back and relaxing setting. The private tastings include pinot noir and chardonnay wines, and seasonal victuals to match.

By appointment only.

## Regusci Winery

*5584 Silverado Trail, Napa, 707-254-0403; www.regusciwinery.com*

This fantastic winery goes way back. In fact, it's one of the few "ghost wineries," a term given to those wineries that were around before 1900. During the 1890s, many vineyards were wiped out because of a phylloxera infestation. However, a few were folded into more modern facilities, one of which was located on the Regusci ranch. In 1932, Gaetano Regusci bought the historic property, at first farming other crops, and it has been a family biz ever

WINE COUNTRY

since. Today, the family only farms grapes, having established the winery in 1996. The tasting room is a real find (we're almost tempted to keep it to ourselves). You'll find some of the best cabernet sauvignon you've ever tasted, as well as merlot, zinfandel and chardonnay.

### Silver Oak Winery
*915 Oakville Cross Road, Oakville, 707-942-7022; www.silveroak.com*
Silver Oak is a favorite among wine enthusiasts who come back year after year to taste the newest cabernet sauvignon. They now have a new winery to visit (a welcome relief if you were at their temporary facility). The Tudor-style estate features a tasting room with a stone fireplace and oak tasting bar with steel barrel hoops, designed to resemble the winery's signature American oak barrels. Many gladly fork over upwards of $100 for a bottle of the dark and velvety cabs. The family also owns **Twomey Cellars** (www.twomeycellars.com), which produces merlot, pinot noir and sauvignon blanc.
Monday-Saturday 9 a.m.-5 p.m.

## STAY

### ★★★The Carneros Inn
*4048 Sonoma Highway, Napa, 707-299-4900; www.thecarnerosinn.com*
Between Napa and Sonoma, and surrounded by vineyards, this inn was designed to resemble the countryside with barns and ranchers' cottages. It looks like a place all the hipsters would live if they had to move to the country—which is exactly the point. The stylish, private cottages offer luxurious accommodations with an array of modern amenities—heated slate floors in the bathrooms, flat-screen televisions and gas fireplaces—and all have large patios (where you can dine alfresco) and indoor/outdoor showers. The restaurant, Farm, packs them in nightly for its fantastic food and wine list, and locals swear by the Boon Fly Café for breakfast—especially for the homemade doughnuts, widely considered the perfect hangover cure.
86 rooms. Wireless Internet access. Two restaurants, two bars. Fitness center. Spa. Pool. Business center. $$$$

# NAPA VALLEY

## EAT

### ★★★Napa Valley Wine Train
*1275 McKinstry St., Napa, 707-253-2111, 800-427-4124; www.winetrain.com*
Ride the "Gourmet Express" for a well-crafted culinary and wine experience. This unusual tour will take you through the heart of the Napa Valley in meticulously restored Pullman dining cars (circa 1915) with luxurious interiors or 1952 Vista Dome cars for an elevated scenic view.
California, French menu. Lunch, dinner. Bar. Children's menu. Business casual attire. Reservations recommended. $$

### Oakville Grocery
*7856 St. Helena Highway, Oakville, 707-944-8802; www.oakvillegrocery.com*
Though frequented by tour buses and carloads of winery-goers, it's still worth a stop if for nothing more than an afternoon latte. Oakville Grocery is considered the place to pack a wine country-worthy picnic with a wide selection of cheese, charcuterie, condiments, sweets and other delicious finds.
Daily 8 a.m.-6 p.m.

*Ubuntu • Napa Soap Company • Napa Valley Wine Train • Napa Valley Opera House*

### Ubuntu
*1140 Main St., Napa, 707-251-5656; www.ubuntunapa.com*
Though you'll find no meat on the menu, the focus at Ubuntu is less on depravity than fresh, innovative cuisine from local community gardens. Named after the Zulu term for "humanity toward others," the space functions as both a vegetarian restaurant and a yoga studio. The open kitchen serves up such succulent dishes as coq au vin with spring vegetables, a deep-fried egg and Lion's Run Cabernet, and toasted bread dumplings with courgettes and basil. Executive chef Jeremy Fox grows most of the restaurant's food on its own biodynamic farm and prepares an eclectic monu of items sure to please even the most stubborn carnivore. And lest you forget you're in Napa Valley: Wine pairings are offered to compliment the nightly garden menu.
Vegetarian menu. Dinner, Saturday-Sunday brunch. Casual attire. $$

## SPA

### ★★★★The Spa at The Carneros Inn
*4048 Sonoma Highway, Napa, 707-299-4900; www.thecarnerosinn.com*
Napa Valley's The Carneros Inn takes the country farmhouse and turns it

NAPA VALLEY WINE TRAIN

OXBOW PUBLIC MARKET

on its head, with clean lines and simple sophistication, and the sun-filled, mood-lifting spa perfectly complements the resort's laid-back attitude. The themed treatment menu draws from the harvests, farms, cellars, minerals and creeks of the Carneros Valley. Therapies include honeydew exfoliations, goat butter body wraps, grape seed and guava body scrubs, and apricot and chardonnay manicures. If you'd rather not leave your private cottage but desperately need a massage, the spa presents a menu of in-room treatments, including organic garden wraps and couples' massages.

## SEE AND DO

### Downtown Napa

Ride a free downtown trolley that passes by several Victorian structures—the city has more pre-1906 Victorians than anywhere else in the Bay Area, which was hit by the big San Francisco earthquake of the same year. The trolley makes stops at COPIA and Napa premium outlets. Napa County Landmarks (707-255-1836) periodically conducts 90-minute guided tours on Saturdays, May through October.

### Napa Valley Opera House

*1030 Main St., Napa, 707-226-7372;*
*www.napavalleyoperahouse.org*
The opera house was built in 1879 as one of the first "respectable" venues west of the Mississippi river. The building went dark in 1914 and was finally renovated and reopened to the public in 2002 after being restored to its former splendor. The show schedule includes everything from jazz and classical concerts to theater and dance productions.

## SHOP

### Oxbow Public Market

*610 First St., Napa, 707-226-6529;*
*www.oxbowpublicmarket.com*
After a day of vineyard hopping, you'll no doubt be exhausted—and hungry. If you're looking for more of a DIY dinner option, head to Oxbow Public Market, a one-stop artisanal food and wine shop located in Napa's up-and-coming Oxbow District. Grab a cup of made-to-order coffee from San Francisco's own Ritual Coffee Roasters, pick up a

NAPA VALLEY

# A DAY OF PRIVATE WINE TASTING

There are essentially two ways to sip your way through northern California's best wineries: go elbow-to-elbow with the masses at the open (and, for that reason, popular) tasting rooms, or make reservations ahead of time and enjoy a more intimate experience. If spontaneity and meeting new friends are priorities, pick a few big name wineries and use the first tactic; but if private indulgence is key, consider the following itinerary:

Start in the Stags Leap District, which is known for its cabernet sauvignon, in lower Napa. Make **Hartwell Vineyards** (*5795 Silverado Trail, 707-255-4269; www.hartwellvineyards.com*) your first stop. You'll see its formidable iron gate and Cyprus tree-lined driveway from the west side of the Silverado Trail. Private tours and tastings ($45 per person) are available Wednesday-Saturday at 11 a.m. and 2 p.m. only. Enjoy cheese, chocolates and generous pours of Hartwell's library wines, available only at the winery.

About a mile north on the same road, look for a turnoff on the east side that is marked only by several numeric addresses—6126 should be among them. Follow the road back into the hills and eventually you'll come upon one of the more unusual architectural masterpieces in the valley. The famed Viennese artist Friedensreich Hundertwasser designed the whimsical **Quixote Winery** (*6126 Silverado Trail, 707-944-2659; www.quixotewinery.com*) with the idea that Napa needed a winery that didn't take itself too seriously. Your private tour ($25 per person) will explain how this brightly colored tile and stucco building—complete with a giant, golden turret—came to be and includes tastings of Quixote's signature petite syrah.

At this point, you're probably getting a little hungry. Make **Robert Sinskey Vineyards** (*6320 Silverado Trail, 707-944-9090; www.robertsinskey.com*) your next stop. Known for its organically farmed vines, this winery takes food pairing seriously. Make a reservation ahead of time for the bento box tasting at noon and enjoy a light, four-course lunch paired with seasonal wines. $60 per person.

For an up close view of another Napa Valley architectural gem, continue on the Silverado Trail to the **Castello di Amorosa** (*4045 North St. Helena Highway, 707-967-6272; www.castellodiamorosa.com*). This 13th century-style Tuscan castle took 14 years to build using hand-chiseled stones sourced locally and in Europe. The details are impressive, like the thousands of handmade bolts for every door, a working well in the courtyard, Italian murals and a massive 500-year-old fireplace. And then there's the wine. The best way to enjoy the castello is the extensive VIP tour, which will take you away from the crowds, through the 107 rooms and deep into the caves beneath the castle to explain the winemaking process as well as the castle's construction. Finish with a private tasting served with a variety of antipasto dishes and fine wines. $500 for two people.

mobiltravelguide.com

WINE COUNTRY

bottle of local wine from Oxbow Wine Merchant, or opt for the fresh-baked bread, house cured meats or newly shucked oysters. Whatever you grab, you can be assured it'll be local, and tasty.

# ANNUAL NAPA VALLEY EVENTS

## FEBRUARY–MARCH

### Napa Valley Mustard Festival

This celebration was first conceived to enliven the valley during the typically slow winter months. But there's nothing particularly wintry about the area in February and March—in fact, the festival is so named because much of the valley is covered in brilliant yellow wild mustard flowers. The now popular celebration includes grand dinners, jazz concerts, art exhibitions, a photography contest and wine tasting. For the current year's schedule of events, go to www.mustardfestival.org

## JULY

### Summer Music Festival at Robert Mondavi Winery

Past concerts have included Ella Fitzgerald, Tony Bennett, Buena Vista Social Club, New Orleans' Preservation Hall Jazz Band and Aimee Mann. Concerts are held July through August and ticket sales begin in April (*www.robertmondaviwinery.com*).

### Wine Country Film Festival

Held over four weekends in July and August, this roving outdoor film festival takes place throughout Napa and Sonoma. Flicks such as *A Fish Called Wanda* and *Honeymoon in Vegas* debuted here, and past celebrity guests such as Gregory Peck, George Lucas and Richard Dreyfuss have dropped by. Tickets range from $7-$15, or $90-$145 for weekend passes (*www.winecountryfilmfest.com*). Wine and gourmet foods are available for purchase.

## AUGUST

### Chamber Music Festival

The annual music-in-the-vineyards three-week Chamber Music Festival features many notable artists-in-residence. Concerts are held at various wineries with tastings at intermission. Tickets on sale in April (*www.napavalleymusic.com*).

## DECEMBER

Traditional Christmas carols are played on rare string, wind and percussion instruments in candlelit intimate wine caves throughout the Napa Valley during the annual carols in the caves festival. Tickets cost $40 (*www.carolsinthecaves.com*).

The Yountville Festival of Lights is a free month-long holiday celebration when quaint Yountville is draped in thousands of tiny lights and residents and visitors linger on the streets to sample culinary treats and wine. Horse-drawn carriages provide transportation on Saturdays.

# CHAPTER 2
# SONOMA VALLEY

*The Lodge at Sonoma Firepit Patio ▪ Lunch at The Fairmont Sonoma Mission Inn & Spa ▪ The Fairmont Sonoma Mission Inn & Spa ▪ The Lodge at Sonoma Pool*

The quieter sister to nearby Napa, Sonoma has plenty of top-notch wineries, luxurious inns and spas, and superlative dining, but without the crowds. The oldest town in the wine region, Sonoma was arranged around the eight-acre plaza like a traditional Mexican village because up until 1846, it was under Mexican rule. On June 14 of that year, a group of settlers rebelled in the so-called "Bear Flag Revolt," and for a brief 25 days, Sonoma was declared the capital of California. The U.S. government then annexed California, ending Sonoma's days as the seat of state government. Today, the history of the town is well preserved. City Hall, built in the heart of the plaza in the early 20th century, is still used and the Franciscan mission **San Francisco Solano** (*114 E. Spain St., 707-938-9560; tours are typically given on the hour between 11 a.m. and 2 p.m. on weekends*), dating back to 1823, is open to the public. In addition to the history, Sonoma's shops and restaurants are well worth the visit. And, of course, there are the famed wineries.

THE FAIRMONT SONOMA MISSION INN AND SPA

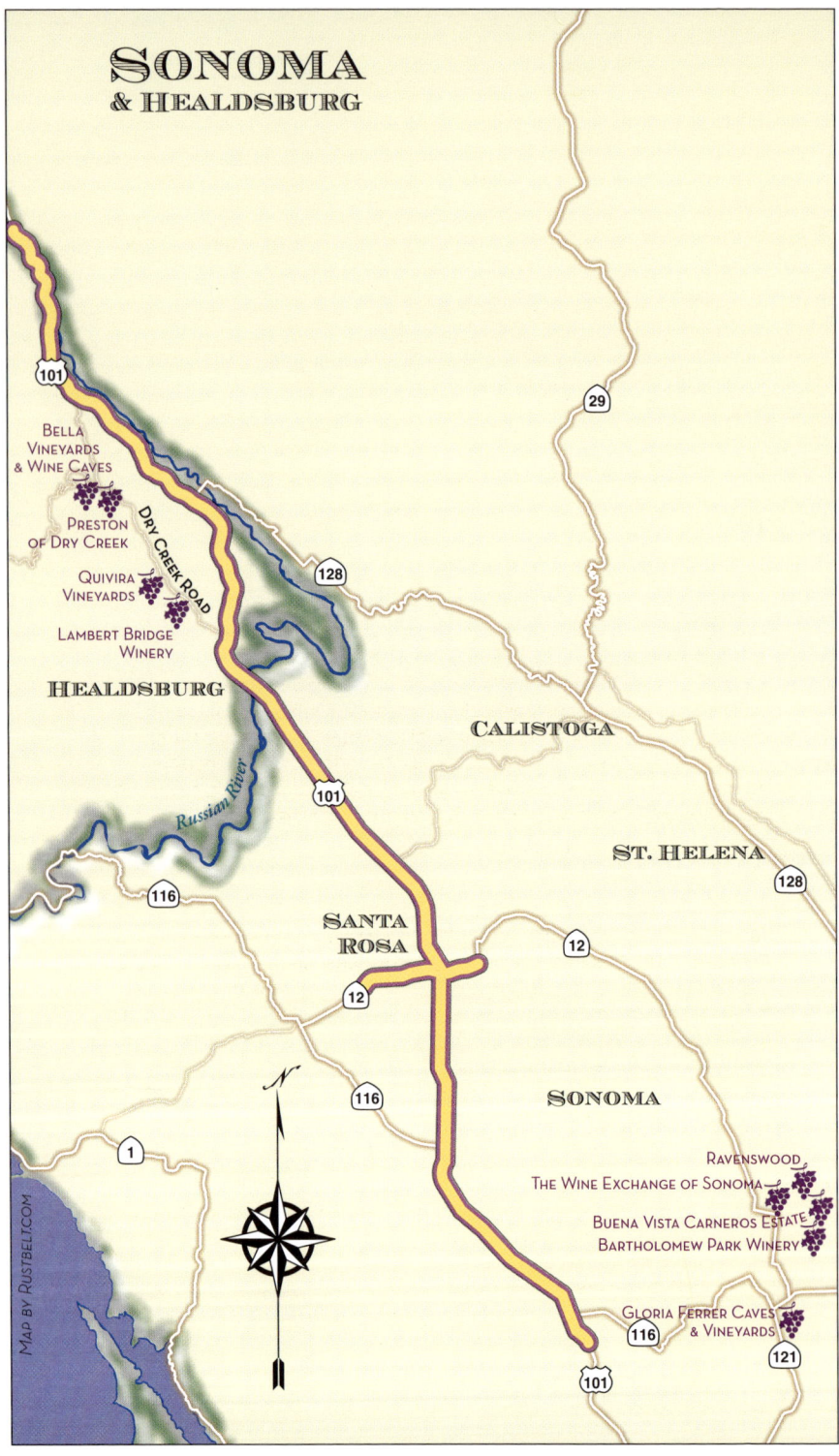

GLORIA FERRER CAVES AND VINEYARDS

# TASTE

### Bartholomew Park Winery
*1000 Vineyard Lane, Sonoma, 707-935-9511; www.bartpark.com*
Grapes have been grown on this land since the 1830s, but Bartholomew Park has existed as a winery only since 1994. With winemaker Jim Bundschu (of the long-time Sonoma family behind nearby Gundlach Bundshcu winery's Rhinefarm) at the helm, expect to find limited-production single vineyard wines that range from soft, full merlots to crisp, refreshing whites. Pick up a picnic in town and plan on a hike through the winery's trails, which on a clear day deliver views across the valley to San Francisco. Afterward, buy a cold bottle of sauvignon blanc from the tasting room and take a seat at one of the picnic tables that overlook the vineyards for an unforgettable lunch.
Daily 11 a.m.-4:30 p.m.

### Buena Vista Carneros Historic Tasting Room
*18000 Old Winery Road, Sonoma, 707-938-1266; www.buenavistacarneros.com*
Founded in 1857, Buena Vista is California's oldest premium winery and a California historic landmark. The 1862 Press House stands as the estate's tasting room, and history buffs will particularly enjoy the tour, as it recounts Buena Vista's past and the life of Count Agoston Haraszthy, the man behind today's winemaking techniques. There are a number of different tasting options—from library vintages to seated food and wine pairings—so be sure to call ahead for details.
Daily 10 a.m.-5 p.m., reservations recommended.

### Gloria Ferrer Caves & Vineyards
*23555 Highway 121 (Arnold Drive), Sonoma, 707-996-7256; www.gloriaferrer.com*
The first sparkling wine house to settle in the Sonoma Carneros region, Gloria Ferrer is an idyllic stop for a glass of Brut Rosé and a nibble on some of their delicious, addicting house-roasted spicy almonds. The daily tours include a peek at century-old winemaking equipment and a journey into the estate's cellar. Unlike other wineries in the area, Gloria Ferrer does not

# SONOMA VALLEY

provide tasting samples; rather they sell their wines by the full glass or bottle. Grab a flute, head out to the sun-drenched Vista Terrace and relax as you overlook the estate vineyards. For those who prefer still wines, Gloria Ferrer also offers a limited-release Pinot Noir Rosé and a variety of more robust pinot noirs.

Daily 10 a.m.-5 p.m.; tour reservations recommended for parties of 10 or more.

### Ravenswood
*18701 Gehricke Road, Sonoma, 707-933-2332; www.ravenswood-wine.com*
This Sonoma winemaker's well-priced zinfandels may be ubiquitous (you can find the vintner's blends in most grocery stores across the U.S.), but they're some of the most robust, deliciously drinkable American reds around. Winemaker Joel Peterson's mantra is "no wimpy wines," and that philosophy shows in the full-bodied wines Ravenswood produces. A visit to the rustic tasting room gives you a chance to sample some of the winery's limited-production vineyard designate zinfandels, all of which are acclaimed

*The El Dorado Kitchen • Sonoma Lavender • Carneros Restaurant • Sonoma Coastline*

for their rich taste (think big flavor with notes ranging from vanilla to cedar to raspberry, depending on the vineyard).
Daily 10 a.m.-4:30 p.m.

## STAY

### ★★El Dorado Hotel
*405 First St. West, Sonoma, 707-996-3220; www.eldoradosonoma.com*
Bringing a sleek, modern alternative to the historic Sonoma Plaza, the El Dorado offers stylish, contemporary rooms with private balconies and views of the town square or lush garden courtyard. The outdoor pool encourages afternoon lounging, and guests don't have to stray far for a world-class meal with El Dorado Kitchen positioned right off the lobby.
27 rooms. Restaurant, bar. Pool. $$

### ★★★The Fairmont Sonoma Mission Inn & Spa
*100 Boyes Blvd., Sonoma, 707-938-9000,800-257-7544;*
*www.fairmont.com/sonoma*
A local favorite since the 1920s, this idyllic country retreat sits on Boyes

Hot Springs—a sacred healing ground for Native Americans—and within the valley's famous vineyards. Many of the sophisticated yet country-comfortable guest rooms have French doors that open to a private patio or balcony. Romantic suites hold fireplaces and four-poster beds. Hearty American fare has been served for more than 50 years at the Big 3 diner, while Santé earns praise for its imaginative cuisine. Relax by the pool or play a round of golf on the historic 1925 course. Inspired by the thermal mineral springs that flow underneath the inn, the spa is a destination unto itself, wowing city slickers with its comprehensive treatment menu. 226 rooms. Wireless Internet access. Five restaurants, three bars. Fitness center. Spa. $$$$

### ★★★MacArthur Place
*29 E. MacArthur St., Sonoma, 800-722-1866; www.macarthurplace.com*
A lush country estate just a few blocks from the town plaza, this magical inn sits among seven acres of fragrant, blooming gardens. The Victorian-style buildings house 64 guest rooms and suites, some with fireplaces and oversized bathrooms that deliver California country charm and comfort. A nightly wine and cheese reception whets the appetite, but save room for the juicy steaks and succulent seafood at Saddles, the hotel's steakhouse. Even in this tranquil setting, the Garden Spa stands out for its sunlit space and local flower-, plant- and herb-based treatments.
64 rooms. Wireless Internet access. Complimentary continental breakfast. Restaurant. $$$

## EAT

### ★★★Carneros Bistro & Wine Bar
*1325 Broadway, Sonoma, 707-931-2042; www.carnerosbistro.com*
About six blocks south of the Sonoma plaza, Carneros is adjacent to the lodge at Sonoma, sharing the circular drive. An extensive wine list, wine bar and wine education classes are offered along with an innovative menu of international fare. An open kitchen runs the length of the dining room. Check for special events and live entertainment and keep an eye out for celebrity bartenders.
International/fusion menu. Breakfast, lunch, dinner, brunch. Bar. Children's menu. Business casual attire. Reservations recommended. Outdoor seating. $$$

EL DORADO KITCHEN

HOT AIR BALOONS IN SONOMA

DOWNTOWN HEALDSBURG

### ★★The Girl and the Fig
*110 W. Spain St., Sonoma, 707-938-3634; www.thegirlandthefig.com*
Prepare yourself for fresh, rustic, French-influenced cooking at this simple, rustic restaurant on Sonoma's town square. The waitstaff can range from affable to absent, but once you dig into dishes such as fig and argula salad with fresh balsamic dressing, or skillet steak with asparagus and truffle mac 'n' cheese, you'll forget about the service. A wine list heavy with local syrahs provides the perfect complement to the California cuisine offered on the constantly changing menu. The outdoor patio is a divine spot to indulge in weekend brunch or a romantic dinner.
California menu. Lunch, dinner, Sunday brunch. Bar. Casual attire. Reservations recommended. Outdoor seating. $$

### Della Santina's
*133 E. Napa St., Sonoma, 707-935-0576; www.dellasantinas.com*
This family-run, old school Italian restaurant is just off Sonoma's main square and displays a palace-like stone exterior that you'd expect to find among the hills of Tuscany. The rosticceria turns out perfectly tender meats, and one bite of Della Santina's signature tiramisu from the pasticceria and you'll be ordering a second helping for a midnight snack. Highlights include the pappardelle alla lepre (wide noodles with rabbit meat sauce) and the daily gnocchi special. In warm weather, vie for a table on the patio.
Italian menu. Lunch, dinner. Outdoor seating. $$

### El Dorado Kitchen
*405 First St. West, Sonoma, 707-996-3030; www.eldoradosonoma.com*
Both sophisticated and simple, dramatic and relaxing, this bustling eatery shows off the understated brilliance of chef Justin Everett's contemporary Californian cuisine, amidst an open kitchen, a long communal dining table and an intimate stone courtyard for dining under the Sonoma sky. Seasonal freshness is the focus and dishes such as free range Petaluma chicken breast with quinoa and squash blossom pesto, and herb-basted halibut with shiitake mushrooms, asparagus and house-cured pancetta, are paired with thoughtful selections from local artisan vintners, including more than

SONOMA VALLEY

20 wines by the glass. If it's more of an afternoon sugar rush that you're after, the neighboring El Dorado Kitchenette has pastries galore, as well as gourmet sandwiches, salads and house made ice cream. Californian menu. Lunch, dinner, Sunday brunch. Bar. Casual attire. Reservations recommended. Outdoor seating. $$$

### Harmony Lounge at the Ledson Hotel
*480 First St. East, Sonoma, 707-996-9779; www.ledsonhotel.com*
Enjoy a light meal of small plates with wine pairings at this grand antique hotel on the plaza. Try the beef carpaccio and duck confit and save room for the pear cabernet tart. Check for live entertainment. American/international menu. Lunch, dinner. Bar. $

## SEE AND SHOP

### The Vasquez House Library and Tea Room
*414 First St. East, Sonoma, 707-938-0510; www.sonomaleague.org*
Find vintage exhibits and extensive photographic and historical archives on Sonoma's history in this house that dates back to 1850. It was originally built for Civil War hero General Joe Hooker. It's now maintained by the local historical society, which serves homemade pastries and tea to visitors. Thursday-Saturday 2-4:30 p.m.

### Vella Cheese Company
*315 Second St. East, Sonoma, 707-938-3232; www.vellacheese.com*
Not much has changed over the past 70 years for this cheese company. Housed in a century-old stone building originally intended for a brewery, it remains a family-run operation that puts quality before all else. Whether you're in the mood for a slice of sharp raw milk cheddar or a wheel of dry monterey jack, locals and visitors will agree that little tastes better with a bottle of local wine than a serving of fresh vella cheese.
Monday-Saturday 9:30 a.m.-6 p.m.

### Tiddle E. Winks
*115 E. Napa St., Sonoma, 707-939-6933; www.tiddleewinks.com*
A veritable tribute to Boomer nostalgia, this delightful boutique is packed with curios and gifts sourced mainly from the 1950s. Here you'll find retro candy dots and traditional ice cream sandwiches alongside vintage diner signs, toys and books.
Daily 11 a.m.-6 p.m., Sundays 11 a.m.-5 p.m.

## HEALDSBURG

In the center of some of Northern California's most esteemed winemaking appellations, including Alexander Valley, Dry Creek, Chalk Hill and Russian River Valley, is the thriving and charming wine town of Healdsburg, where palm trees and 100-year old redwoods shade manicured grounds and benches in the town square. The town of Healdsburg is centrally located with access to more than 70 world-class wineries, from the grandest European-style villas to the more rustic, yet no less well-crafted mom-and-pop shops. Just outside of town is one of the most beautiful drives in Northern California—Dry Creek Road—home to many of the area's wineries. Its windy turns provide a leisurely way to spend an afternoon as you hop from one tasting to the next.

mobiltravelguide.com

## SONOMA VALLEY

## TASTE

### Bella Vineyards and Wine Caves
*9711 W. Dry Creek Road, Healdsburg, 866-572-3552; www.bellawinery.com*
It's the classic tale: Girl meets boy. Girl marries boy. Couple moves to wine country and learns how to make wine. Classic or not, few could pull it off like Scott and Lynn Adams, earning accolades for producing some of the best wine in the region. Bella harvests a varied crop of wines from its three distinct vineyards in the Dry Creek and Alexander valleys, including zinfandel and syrahs. While the wines are certainly top-notch, a big reason for Bella's appeal is its beautiful caves. Entering on the side of a hill underneath an arbor of vines, you'll be given a glimpse into the inner workings of the winery, as well as an underground taste or two.
Daily 11 a.m.- 4:30 p.m.

### Lambert Bridge Winery
*4085 W. Dry Creek Road, Healdsburg, 707-431-9600; www.lambertbridge.com*
The beauty of visiting Lambert Bridge Winery is best summed up in its mission statement: "Great wine served with great food shared by great friends." When you visit the family-run vineyard, located in the heart of the Dry Creek Valley, you will immediately recognize its commitment to this vision. The well-manicured grounds and gardens bursting with edible flowers and herbs offer teak tables and chairs for enjoying an impromptu alfresco picnic and a bottle of the Lambert Bridge 2006 Viognier. Or take your visit a bit further by joining chef Andrea Mugnaini in the stunning outdoor kitchen for a class on wood-fired cooking, before feasting on your creations and wines to match.
Daily 10:30 a.m.-4:30 p.m.

### Preston of Dry Creek
*9282 W. Dry Creek Road, Healdsburg, 707-433-3372; www.prestonvineyards.com*
It's all about self-sustainability at this small, family-run winery in the Dry Creek Valley. Owned by Lou and Susan Preston for more than three decades, the wines are made from organically grown grapes, and the selection of fresh produce sold from an ad hoc stand on the front porch is also organic. Preston epitomizes down-home charm, with weather-worn farmhouses dotting the estate and a verdant yard with picnic tables and bocci courts for visitors to enjoy. Grab a loaf of house made bread, some local cheese and a bottle of their crisp Vin Gris Rosé and relax under a canopy of lemon trees.
Daily 11 a.m.-4:30 p.m.

### Quivira Vineyards
*4900 W. Dry Creek Road, Healdsburg, 707-431-8333; www.quivirawine.com*
Just down the road from Lambert Bridge Winery in the heart of the Dry Creek Valley, this innovative estate is committed to organic and biodynamic winemaking practices, transforming the once wood-and-cinder barn into a solar-paneled, high-tech edifice. Reds are the specialty here, with such smooth varietals as the 2006 Steelhead Zinfandel, a robust blend named after the wild trout that spawn in the onsite creek each year. On a hot day, the sauvignon blanc is a real treat, especially under the shade of Quivira's ancient fig trees.
Daily 11 a.m.-5 p.m.

## STAY

### ★★★Hotel Healdsburg
*25 Matheson St., Healdsburg, 707-431-2800; www.hotelhealdsburg.com*
The Hotel Healdsburg is a hip oen-

HOTEL HEALDSBURG

ophile's dream. This striking, contemporary hotel right on the historic Town Plaza is a showpiece of minimalist design. The clean lines and uncluttered décor create a serene ambience throughout the public spaces, and the guest rooms and suites echo that sentiment. Windows look out over the plaza or toward the hotel's garden. All of wine country is easily explored from here, but the property is a culinary destination of its own, with noted chef Charlie Palmer's lauded Dry Creek Kitchen.
55 rooms. High-speed Internet access. Complimentary continental breakfast. Restaurant, bar. Fitness center. Spa. Pool. Business center. $$$$

### ★★★Les Mars Hotel
*27 North St., Healdsburg, 707-433-4211; www.lesmarshotel.com*
Imagine the thrill of staying with close friends while on vacation. Now take that thought and add a bucolic wine country setting, a classic chateau-style residence and peerless attention to detail. Located on a side street just off the main strip, the hotel boasts 16 rooms individually decorated with antiques and luxurious linens. The hand-carved walnut-panel library offers a tranquil respite after a day of wine tastings, and the delicious complimentary breakfast delivered to your room each morning will make you think twice about ever staying with friends again.
16 rooms. Wireless Internet access. Complimentary breakfast. Pool. $$$$

## EAT

### ★★★★Cyrus
*29 North St., Healdsburg, 707-433-3311; www.cyrusrestaurant.com*
Where better to indulge in life's luxuries than this elegant wine country eatery located off the lobby of the grand Les Mars Hotel? Leather banquettes, a cloister ceiling and a plethora of freshly cut flowers are just some of the intimate touches that make an evening at Cyrus a sybaritic affair. Start off with one of the restaurant's famous house made specialty cocktails or enjoy a glass of champagne and a bite of caviar from their champagne and caviar cart rolled to you tableside. The prix fixe menu of three, four or five courses changes daily, but often includes such scrumptious dishes as roasted porcini risotto and rabbit ballotine, and a terrine of foie gras

# SONOMA VALLEY

rhubarb and sassafrass. The wine list of more than 600-bottles offers a perfect accompaniment to any dish.
Continental menu. Dinner. Bar. Business casual attire. Reservations recommended. Credit cards accepted. $$$$

### ★★Dry Creek Kitchen
*317 Healdsburg Ave., Healdsburg, 707-431-0330*
Housed in the modern Hotel Healdsburg, the Dry Creek Kitchen suits many tastes. Sit outside in the morning with your latte and watch the town wake up, or settle inside and enjoy an exercise in rustic comfort, with down-home dishes and a waitstaff that's all smiles. Be sure to remember a bottle of local wine too, as the restaurant does not charge a corkage fee for up to two bottles of local vino.
American menu. Dinner. Bar. Business casual attire. Reservations recommended. Outdoor seating. $$$

Hotel Healdsburg • Bella Vineyards and Wine Caves • Hotel Healdsburg • Dry Creek Kitchen

### Scopa
*109A Plaza St., Healdsburg, 707-433-5282; www.scopahealdsburg.com*
For those who have spent half their lives longing for an Italian grandmother, one trip to Scopa and you'll have found the only Nonna you'll need. A newcomer to the gourmet playground that is wine country, this sliver of an Italian bistro has an intimate white marble bar and unassuming interior. The food, however, is simple and delicious. Chef and owner Ari Rosen churns out house made gnocchi with a Napolitano meat ragu and a spectacular moscardini of sauteed baby octopus with Yukon potatoes and caper berries. The wine list is thorough and surprisingly reasonable—by wine country standards—and if you can't find anything of your liking, bring your own bottle along (there's a $20 corkage fee).
Italian menu. Dinner. Closed Monday. $$$

## SHOP

### 14feet.
*325 Center St., Healdsburg, 707-433-3391; www.14feet.net*
The term vintage is thrown around a lot in Healdsburg, but the folks at

14feet. aren't talking about the grape variety. This storefront, specializing in one-of-a-kind industrial and mid-century pieces, is choc-a-block full of vintage tables, chairs, light fixtures, antique textiles and even an oversized ceramic peanut bank from the 70s. You never know what you'll find, but there's little chance you'll go home empty-handed.
Monday-Saturday 10 a.m-6 p.m., Sunday 11 a.m.-5 p.m.

### Lime Stone

*315 Healdsburg Ave., Healdsburg, 707-433-3080; www.limestonehealdsburg.com*
This colorful corner shop housed in the Hotel Healdsburg is owned by Charlie and Lisa Palmer of nearby Dry Creek Kitchen, and reigns as Healdsburg's go-to for chic home accents. Take home a wine barrel chandelier, ox-cart table, classic glass candlesticks or petite porcelain pear vases to remind you of your fabulous vacation.
Monday-Tuesday 10 a.m.-6 p.m., Wednesday-Thursday 10 a.m.-7 p.m., Friday-Saturday 10 a.m.-8 p.m., Sunday 10 a.m.-7 p.m.

### Myra Hoefer Design

*309 Healdsburg Ave., 707-433-2166; www.myrahoeferdesign.com*
The store's namesake is as colorful a personality as you'll find in Sonoma. Her impeccable and eccentric Parisian chic taste is evident in the limited, but well-edited selection of antique furnishings, books and knick-knacks.
Monday-Friday noon-4 p.m., Saturday-Sunday noon-5 p.m.

# CHAPTER 3
# CENTRAL COAST

*Chateau Julien • Sunflowers at Earthbound Farms • The Hungry Cat • Alma Rosa Tasting Room*

The Central Coast is a large wine region, stretching from the Santa Cruz Mountains to Santa Barbara. There are many fantastic trips to be had here, including the one that begins with a stop in Carmel and a visit to Santa Barbara. You'll be amazed at how good—and affordable—the wines are in this area. You'll pay an arm and a leg for lodging in either locale, but you'll be shipping home boxes of wine for a steal. You'll also get an opportunity to sample the wines of up-and-coming winemakers whose bottles you can't find anywhere else. Unlike Napa, the vineyard owners in the Central Coast area haven't reached the mega-successes of a Mondavi or Gallo. Many are the kind of hard-working and independent Californians you'll be happy to know still exist—like the family that runs Boëté, which produces about 1,500 cases a year. A bottle of their divine cheval rouge sells for only $30. Other winemakers in this area are well-rounded people whose successes stretch far beyond producing great wine. They'll share their stories when you pull up a seat at their tasting rooms—like the one about the racecar driver-turned winemaker at Bernardus, whose father one day drew a sketch that eventually became the template for the VW bus. Or the guy at Parsonage who was once in counterintelligence and now makes great pinot. These are the sorts of stories that make wine tasting an even more pleasurable activity than it is by itself, and you'll hear lots of them on this trip.

FOUR SEASONS BILTMORE SANTA BARBARA

MORGAN WINERY

## CARMEL

What's known simply as "Carmel" is divided into the town (officially called "Carmel-by-the-Sea") and Carmel Valley Village, about 13 miles inland. The former, whose famous mayor was Clint Eastwood, almost looks like a movie set. It's that perfect—some say too perfect. You can disdain it the way you would prom queens or Martha Stewart, or you can happily do as thousands of others do and enjoy its white sandy beaches and peruse its tidy shops, which are so pristine they don't even have the clutter of street addresses. The town's center runs the length of Ocean Avenue, which takes you from Highway 1 all the way to the dead end at Carmel Beach, and provides luxurious accommodations and plenty of restaurants. The valley is more dusty and sleepy, but you're closer to the tasting rooms and there are equally nice places to stay.

## TASTE

### Bernardus Winery
*5 West Carmel Valley Road, Carmel Valley, 831-659-1900, 800-223-2533; www.bernardus.com*
Owner Ben Pon's father designed the VW bus (see his original sketch inside the restaurant in the lodge). Pon himself raced Porsches, and since the 1970s, he's been (warning: cheesy pun ahead) putting the peddle to the meddle making furious wines. With vineyards located in the Cachagua region of the Carmel Valley, Bernardus produces beautiful cabernets, chardonnays, merlots and more. But the trophy goes to Marinus Estate's Bordeaux-style wine, a rich, full-bodied wine with a long finish (at Bernardus, it's all about the mouth feel). The blend includes a heady mix of cabernet sauvignon, merlot, cabernet franc, petit verdot and malbec. Definitely don't plan on driving if this is your last stop.
Daily 11 a.m.-5 p.m. Groups of eight or more should make a reservation.

### Boëté Winery
*Valley Hills Center, 7156 Carmel Valley Road, Carmel Valley, 831-625-5040; www.boetewinery.com*
Owners John and Jana Saunders (Boëté is the last name of John's grand-

CHATEAU JULIEN

parents) and their four sons (Jesse, a bull rider in his free time, manages the tiny tasting room) grow what many say is some of the best fruit in the valley. It must be true because these wines were our favorite. With such a small production (only about 1,500 cases are produced a year), you'll want to join their wine club (we did) and keep the cabernet sauvignon, cabernet franc and the spicy cheval rouge blend coming year-round.
Thursday-Friday 2-5:45 p.m., Saturday-Sunday noon-5:45 p.m.

### Chateau Julien Winery
*8940 Carmel Valley Road, Carmel, 831-624-2600; www.chateaujulien.com*
This 25-year old winery looks like it was plucked from France and set between the town of Carmel and the village. In fact, the estate is modeled after an actual home on the French-Swiss border. The mountains loom in the background and paths are lined with enormous rose bushes. Inside, everyone gathers around a large mahogany table in the great hall to taste and mingle. The winery is known for its merlot. Be sure to scoop up a bottle of the Bravura, a special 25th-anniversary release bordeaux blend that's only sold here. If you're packing a picnic lunch, the patio is a good spot to enjoy it.
Monday-Friday 8 a.m.-5 p.m., Saturday-Sunday 11 a.m.-5 p.m.

### Georis Winery
*4 Pilot Road and Carmel Valley Road, Carmel Valley, 831-659-1050; www.georiswine.com*
This tasting room, built in a circa-1938 adobe building with surrounding gardens filled with wine bottle sculptures, has a hippy-chic feel. The owner, Walter Georis, was in the band, The Sandals, which did the soundtrack for the movie *Endless Summer*. He also owns the art gallery across the street. The winery produces full-bodied cabernet sauvignon and merlot, which are aged for 18 months in the barrel and then for another year in the bottle before being released. Tastings come with cheese and crackers, and groups tend to linger—loudly—on the patio.
Daily 11 a.m.-5 p.m.

# CENTRAL COAST

## Heller Estate

*69 W. Carmel Valley Road, Carmel Valley, 831-659-6220; www.hellerestate.com*
These 100 percent certified-organic vineyards produce wines that do indeed "dance on your palate," as the tag line for this estate proclaims. The vineyard uses several methods for controlling bothersome insects without resorting to chemical sprays, including planting French prune trees, which attract wasps that attack the insects. The winery produces about 25,000 cases annually, a sizeable amount for this area. The cabernets are big and rich with berry flavors. Try the cabernet franc; this bold, medium-body wine has layers of black currants, coriander and black pepper, sweet oak and vanilla. The chardonnays are bright and citrusy, and they have a strong mouthfeel.
Monday-Thursday 11 a.m.-5:30 p.m., Friday-Sunday 11 a.m.-6 p.m.

*Strawberries at the Farmers Market ▪ Wine Tasting at Chateau Julien ▪ Tasting Room at Joullian ▪ Joullian's vineyards*

## Joullian Vineyards

*2 Village Drive, Carmel Valley, 831-659-8100, 866-659-8101; www.joullian.com*
This tasting room, designed to look like an old stone church, is the ideal setting for sampling this winery's approachable wines (the motto here is "serious wines that are fun to drink"). Owner Dick Sias planted the first zinfandel in Carmel Valley and the current Joullian zin is blended with a bit of cabernet and petite sirah as well as alicante bouchet, carignane and grenache. They also grow and produce award-winning cabernet, chardonnay, cabernet franc, and syrah.
Daily 11 a.m.-5 p.m.

## Morgan Winery

*204 Crossroads Blvd., Carmel, 831-626-3700; www.morganwinery.com*
The staff at this tasting room located in the Carmel Crossroads Shopping Village is warm and friendly. In business since 1982, the owners, Donna and Daniel Morgan Lee, open up their library on Sundays so you can taste some of their older wines (we tried a wonderful 1993 Pinot Noir "Reserve Carneros" on a recent visit, and took home three bottles). The Double L

TALBOTT VINEYARDS

vineyard, short for double luck in honor of their twin girls, is located in the northern Santa Lucia Highlands overlooking the Salinas Valley and produces pinot noir, chardonnay and syrah.
Daily 11 a.m.-6 p.m.

### Parsonage
*19 East Carmel Valley Road, Carmel Valley, 831-659-2215; www.parsonagewine.com*
The Parsons seem like two people you'd love to be seated next to at a dinner party. You didn't hear it from us, but word around the copper bar in the winery's new tasting room has it that Bill Parsons was in counterintelligence before turning to grapes. Mary Ellen, his wife, is an artist who makes interesting quilt art, which is on display here. How exactly they got into the wine biz is a little fuzzy—by the time the story was told during our visit, we were well into the excellent syrah, cabernet sauvignon and merlot.
Thursday-Monday 11 a.m.-6 p.m.

### Talbott Vineyards
*53 West Carmel Valley Road, Carmel Valley, 831-659-3500; www.talbottvineyards.com*
This winery was begun by Robert Talbott, Sr. and his wife Audrey, who on trips to Europe to buy silk for their luxury tie company (not to be confused with Talbot's, the major clothing retailer) gained an appreciation for fine wines. In 1982, they planted the 24-acre Diamond T Estate Vineyard and built the first winery in the Carmel Valley. Today, the Talbotts are known for their chardonnay and, in

BERNARDUS LODGE

## A TASTE OF MONTEREY

*700 Cannery Row, Monterey, 831-646-5446; www.tasteofmonterey.com*
This large space overlooking Monterey Bay and only a block from the aquarium is a good place to enjoy many different local wines all in one shot. It has table seating, food, views and lots of vino (from more than 75 producers). More important, it beats driving around back roads getting lost. Spend the entire day here and then walk to one of the many restaurants on Cannery Row.
Daily 11 a.m.-6 p.m.

CENTRAL COAST

## ALL ABOARD

Why drive when someone else will? There are a couple of ways to make your way around the area's tasting rooms without having to get behind the wheel.

The new **Grapevine Express** (www.mst.org), which runs from Monterey to the Carmel Valley, makes several stops along the way, including at the Barnyard Shopping Center (where you'll find Morgan), the Valley Hills Shopping Center (Boëté), Chateau Julien and Carmel Valley Village. The service, operated by Monterey-Salinas Transit (it's no party bus but it'll get you around) is so new that some hotel concierges don't even know how it operates. Here's the deal: a day pass costs $4.50, and stops at a place every hour from 11 a.m. to 6 p.m. (so if you get off at Chateau Julien at, say, 11:41, another bus will be by at 12:41 to pick you up). The last return trip to Monterey leaves at 7:15 p.m.

The **Wine Trolley** (831-624-1700; www.toursmonterey.com) is a five-hour tour that hits several wineries including Boëté, Chateau Julien, Bernardus, Heller Estate, Joullian Vineyards and Parsonage. Pickup is at the Portola Plaza in Monterey.

fact, often provide the wine for White House dinners. You'll recognize the Diamond T Chardonnay by its golden straw color, nutty aroma and creamy texture. The tasting room, built to resemble the Talbotts' home, is quite the scene later in the day.
Daily 11 a.m.-5 p.m.

## STAY
### CARMEL VALLEY
#### ★★★★Bernardus Lodge
*415 Carmel Valley Road, Carmel Valley, 831-658-3400; www.bernardus.com*
This homey country lodge is set among acres of vineyards in the Carmel Valley. The minute you walk in, someone hands you a glass of wine and whisks you to your room, bypassing that pesky check-in process, where more wine and snacks (all complimentary) await. The rooms with fireplaces, seating areas and large tubs for two are a bit basic for the price, but they're large and comfortable, and the location, just two miles from the area's tasting rooms, can't be beat. The onsite restaurant, Marinus, is known for organic, seasonal fare.
57 rooms. Wireless Internet access. Two restaurants, bar. Fitness center. Spa. Pool. Tennis. Airport transportation available. Business center. $$$$

MISSION RANCH

### ★★★Quail Lodge Resort & Golf Club
*8205 Valley Greens Drive, Carmel, 831-624-2888, 888-828-8787; www.quaillodge.com*
Set on 850 acres on the sunny side of Carmel Valley, the resort's grounds include rolling hills, lakes and gardens. If you're into golf, you'll love the 18-hole course designed by Robert Muir Graves and the seven-acre driving range. You'll also find three tennis courts, two outdoor pools and a spa offering facials, massages and salon services. (But you might just end up in your room with a buzz watching the plasma TV.) When you're hungry, one of the restaurants, The Covey, has a pretty lakeside setting and offers gourmet cuisine and lots more wine.
97 rooms. High-speed Internet access. Two restaurants, three bars. Airport transportation available. $$$$

## CARMEL-BY-THE-SEA

### ★★★Cypress Inn
*Lincoln Lane and Seventh Street, Carmel, 831-624-3871, 800-443-7443; www.cypress-inn.com*
Built in 1929, this landmark Mediterranean-style hotel is only steps from the town center's boutiques, art galleries and great restaurants. A courtyard off the main lobby welcomes dogs and cats, and the inn also offers pet-sitting services. (Hollywood actress and animal advocate Doris Day is a co-owner.) Guest rooms, which occupy two floors, are not particularly spacious, but they come with thoughtful touches such as pet blankets, fresh flowers, fruit bowls and sherry decanters. Book a deluxe room for more space.
44 rooms. Complimentary continental breakfast. High-speed Internet access. Restaurant, bar. Fitness center. $$

### ★★★Highlands Inn, A Hyatt Hotel
*120 Highlands Drive, Carmel, 831-620-1234; www.highlandsinn.hyatt.com*
Open since 1917, this chic mountain lodge set on a hillside overlooking the surf and Point Lobos has amazing views and a neutral, contemporary design, with wood-burning fireplaces and balconies in most rooms. Book the spa suite for extra rest and relaxation—the two-story suite has a large

# CENTRAL COAST

soaking tub. Otherwise, hit the three outdoor garden spas, perfect after a day of traversing the area's tasting rooms, most of which are only 10 minutes away.

48 rooms. Wireless Internet access. Two restaurants, two bars. Business center. $$$$

### ★★★Mission Ranch
*26270 Dolores St., Carmel, 831-624-6436, 800-538-8221; www.missionranchcarmel.com*

This 1850s farmhouse has had quite a history: it was a creamery, officers club, farmhouse and dance club. Clint Eastwood scooped it up in 1986 when developers wanted to turn it into a condominium development and went about restoring each building to match its original architecture. Today, the ranch is a quiet, rustic place to stay for those who prefer quilts on the bed and open meadows to plasma TVs and mini-bars.

31 rooms. Complimentary continental breakfast. Restaurant, bar. Fitness center. $$

### L'Auberge
*Monte Verde Street at Seventh Avenue, Carmel-by-the-Sea, 831-624-8578; www.laubergecarmel.com*

Spend a romantic weekend at this tiny hotel—only 20 guest rooms—on a quiet street right off the main drag in Carmel-by-the-Sea, where no kids are allowed and the restaurant, Aubergine, is the place to go for an exquisite, boozy meal. Built in 1929, the three-story wood-and-stucco inn was given a major makeover in 2004, giving it that perfect old-meets-new vibe. Guest rooms have jewel tones, coved plaster walls, LCD TVs and heated bathroom floors. The service is superb. Book the sitter.

20 rooms. Complimentary continental breakfast. $$$$

# EAT
## CARMEL VALLEY
### ★★Baja Cantina Grill and Filling Station
*7166 Carmel Valley Road, Carmel, 831-625-2252; www.bajacantinacarmel.com*

Take a break from sniffing for berry, tasting for smoke and figuring out tannin structure. This popular Mexican joint is where the locals head for the killer margaritas and satisfying grub like mango enchiladas and fresh catch tacos. There's live music on the weekends.

Mexican menu. Lunch, dinner. $$

### ★★Café Rustica
*10 DelFino Place, Carmel Valley, 831-659-4444; www.caferusticacarmel.com*

This warm café serves delicious dishes with ingredients that taste like they were picked from the garden only moments ago, and is just the kind of sustenance you need after hours on the wine trail. Thin-crust wood-fired pizzas arrive at your table on a wood plank, bubbling hot and radiating fresh basil. The menu also includes lush salads (such as the BLT with butter lettuce, maple smoked bacon, tomatoes, red onion, house made garlic croutons and Dijon vinaigrette); suppers like the herb-roasted half chicken with crispy artichokes and au gratin potatoes; and specials such as the oh-so-gooey and comforting three-cheese lasagna with mozzarella, ricotta, parmesan and a brilliant marina and pesto sauce. We'd tell you to save room for a dessert like orange croissant bread pudding, but chances are you won't—the food is just too hearty and good.

Country menu. Lunch, dinner. Closed Monday. $$

EARTHBOUND FARMS

### ★★★The Covey
*8205 Valley Greens Drive, Carmel, 831-620-8860, 888-828-8787; www.quaillodge.com*
When you're in California, all the restaurants start to sound the same: fresh, seasonal ingredients procured from local farms. Fortunately, that way of life, er, eating, which began in California, doesn't grow tiresome in practice, at least when the restaurant gets it right. At this fine restaurant overlooking a lake, you'll find dishes like Sonoma duck with gnocchi, and red snapper with lobster ravioli, as well as that mandatory long and intriguing wine list to make things perfect. Or simply stop in from 5-6 p.m. for tapas and wine.
California menu. Breakfast, dinner. Closed Sunday-Monday. Bar. Business casual attire. Reservations recommended. Valet parking. Outdoor seating. $$$

### ★★★★Marinus
*415 Carmel Valley Road, Carmel Valley, 831-658-3595; www.bernardus.com*
Dishes are prepared using organic and fresh ingredients—in fact, neighbors often stop by with extra tomatoes or fishermen come in with their catch of the day. Chef Cal Stamenov then turns the goods into lush salads and main courses such as salmon with English peas, braised leek and buerre blanc. Service is friendly, if a bit chatty, and the huge wine list is certainly impressive, even in wine country.
California menu. Dinner. Business casual attire. Reservations recommended. Valet parking. $$$$

### Earthbound Farms
*7250 Carmel Valley Road, Carmel, 831-625-6219; www.ebfarm.com*
A major player in the produce field—their products are in 75 percent of all supermarkets—Earthbound Farms started in 1984, producing herbs and a variety of organic greens for restaurants in the area. Their pre-washed salads put them on the map and the rest is history. The 30 acres in Carmel are devoted to research and development these days, the fruits of which are sold at the farm stand right up front. You'll find pink lemons, golden raspberries, multi-colored beets (prepared in a delicious salad) and, of

# CENTRAL COAST

course, more than 60 varieties of lettuce. They also sell foamy lattes, warm panini sandwiches, freshly baked breads, sweet treats and more.
Monday-Saturday 8 a.m.-6:30 p.m., Sunday 9 a.m.-6 p.m.

## CARMEL

### Aubergine
*Monte Verde Street at Seventh Avenue, Carmel-by-the-Sea, 831-625-6500; www.laubergecarmel.com*
When dining in this restaurant in the L'Auberge hotel, you might feel like you're in some tiny, out-of-the-way, no-name restaurant in Europe. There are only 12 tables; it's open for only a few hours at a time; and farmers often drop off the ingredients in the morning for that night's dinner. The underground wine cellar has more than 4,000 bottles and each evening, you can choose between three, four and five courses, or simply put yourself in the chef's masterful hands and let him surprise you.
Continental menu. Lunch, dinner. Bar. Business casual attire. Reservations recommended. $$

*Mission Ranch • The Covey • Earthbound Farms • Salad at Marinus*

### Bouchee
*Mission Street, between Ocean and Seventh Avenues, Carmel-by-the-Sea, 831-626-7880; www.boucheecarmel.com*
Head to this sister restaurant to Aubergine for that perfect meal of grilled steak, a mound of frites and a rich glass of red. This more casual modern bistro with an à la carte menu serves all the satisfying classics, while the wine bar next door offers tastings, as well flights and a full wine list. Heck, you could spend an entire evening between the two.
Bistro menu. Dinner. Bar. Casual attire. $

### The Cheese Shop
*Ocean and Junipero Avenues, Carmel Plaza, Carmel-by-the Sea, 831-625-2272; www.cheeseshopinc.com*
The dudes behind the counter at this iconic cheese shop are knowledgeable (they talk about Ewephoria—a sheep's milk cheese from Holland—as casually as the weather) and just plain cool (one rode from Carmel to Seattle on his bike with a wheel of gouda in his backpack). Buy as much as you can stash in your bag for your wine tasting tours, or have them prepare a plate, with whatever condiments you favor, to eat at one of the outdoor ta-

HYDROTHERAPY TUB AT BERNARDUS LODGE

SANTA BARBARA

bles. The small bar in the back offers wine tastings starting at a buck.
Monday-Saturday 10 a.m.-6p.m., Sunday 11 a.m.-5:30 p.m.

### Club Jalapeño
*Between Fifth and Sixth Avenues on San Carlos Street, Carmel-by-the-Sea, 831-626-1997; www.clubjalapeno.com*
After a few rounds of fine dining, you may just want to eat something fried, not organically grown. Dig into chips and salsa, a mound of guacamole and some seriously tasty chicken tortilla soup at this super-satisfying Mexican restaurant. Then order the specialty—the Oaxaca enchiladas. You'll be mopping up every last drop of this spicy, rich sauce, and still eating the rice, beans and ensalada that come on the side. You'll leave feeling like a piñata but it's not every day you find this kind of good Mexican food.
Mexican menu. Lunch (Wednesday-Monday), dinner. Casual attire. $$

## SPA

### ★★★★The Spa at Bernardus Lodge
*415 Carmel Valley Road, Carmel Valley, 831-658-3560, 888-648-9463; www.bernardus.com*
After a good day (or two) of tasting, it's time to clean out the liver and—prepare for more! (You've still got another leg in Santa Barbara.) Book the Vineyard Romance treatment, which includes a harvest crush body exfoliation, lavender-grape seed bath, warm grape seed oil massage and a tea service of grape seed herbal tea. Or try the Chardonnay Facial, an 80-minute, hydrating treatment that incorporates chardonnay grape seeds, which are loaded with antioxidants. It may not do much for your liver, but you'll feel (and look) much better.

## SANTA BARBARA

Ever since Miles Raymond stumbled around this wide-open, folksy wine country in the movie *Sideways*, people have been coming to this region in search of the perfect pinot. The film may have put the area on the wine map, but Santa Barbara has been producing great wines for decades, and not just pinot noir—although that volatile varietal wine is undoubtedly king (thanks to the marine air and cool climate). We recommend staying in Santa Barbara

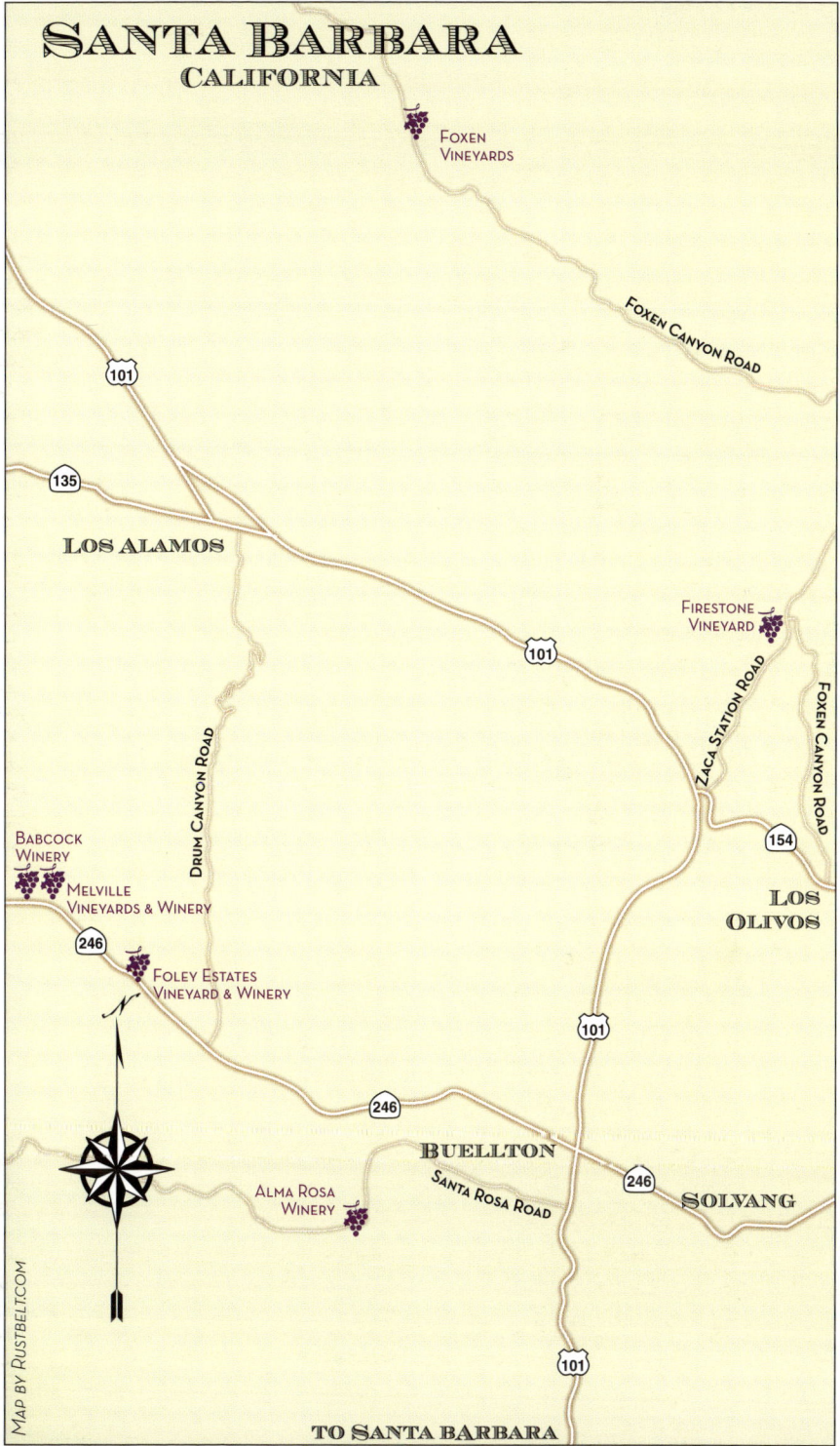

ALMA ROSA

and making the 50-minute drive to the area's wineries along the Foxen and Santa Rita Hills wine trails, and around the tiny town of Los Olivos. It's a bit of a hike, but the trip is scenic, and more important, you'll find luxe accommodations, great restaurants and lots of shopping along State Street in Santa Barbara to round out your trip. To paraphrase Miles, we're gonna drink a lot of good wine and eat some great food, mes frères.

## TASTE

### Alma Rosa Winery
*7250 Santa Rosa Road, Buellton, 805-688-9090; www.almarosawinery.com*
Owner Richard Sanford, formerly a geography major at University of California at Berkeley, is a real maverick, having planted the first pinot noir vines here in 1970. In 2005, he started Alma Rosa with his wife, Thekla. Located on the Rancho Santa Rosa, the vineyards are certified organic and produce chardonnay and pinot noir, as well as pinot gris, pinot blanc and dry pinot noir rosé.
Daily 11 a.m.-4:30 p.m.

### Babcock Winery
*5175 E. Highway 246, Lompoc, 805-736-1455; www.babcockwinery.com*
Brian Babcock is a wine rock star, anointed one of the top ten small production wine makers in the world—the only one in the U.S.—by the James Beard Foundation. The winery produces chardonnay, pinot noir, pinot grigio, sauvignon blanc, syrah and a very good cabernet sauvignon. Babcock also has been experimenting with Italian and Spanish varietals, which he believes will be the next big thing in California winemaking.
Daily 10:30 a.m.-4 p.m.

CENTRAL COAST

### Firestone Vineyard
*5000 Zaca Station Road, Los Olivos, 805-688-3940; www.firestonewine.com*
Firestone has been around since 1972, making it one of the original wineries in Santa Barbara. It sits on a hilltop like the grande dame it is and merits a visit just to admire the pretty location and tasting room. It's also the place to take a tour if you'd like to see the workings of at least one area vineyard (you also learn how the Firestone family went from tires to grapes, which you're almost certainly dying to know). The winery, now owned by Bill Foley, produces chardonnay, cabernet sauvignon, merlot, sauvignon blanc and syrah.
Daily 10 a.m.-5 p.m. Tours start at 11:15 a.m., 1:15 p.m. and 3:15 p.m.

### Foley Estates Vineyard & Winery
*6121 E. Highway 246, Lompoc, 805-737-6222; foleywines.com*
In 1998, Bill Foley purchased land on the Rancho Santa Rosa because of its south-facing hillside and limestone soil, key for producing pinot. Since then, he's built something of a wine empire, acquiring Las Hermanas Vineyard (formerly Ashley's Vineyard) and Firestone, and starting Merus in the Napa Valley to make cabernets. (In his other life, Foley is the chairman of the board of Fidelity.) The large tasting room is located next to the winery building.
Daily 10 a.m.-5 p.m.

### Foxen Vineyards
*7200 Foxen Canyon Road, Santa Maria, 805-937-4251; www.foxenvineyards.com*
This popular winery—the wine club is full—is known for its *Sideways* connection (its tasting room made a brief appearance). Often the tasting room is the only place to taste Foxen's limited release wines. There's plenty to make you happy here, including the lemony chardonnay with vanilla, oak and passionfruit accents, and the plummy merlot, which has a cigar box finish. The tasting room has been described as rustic; it's actually just a shack way up the road on Foxen Canyon, but that's part of the charm.
Daily 11 a.m.-4 p.m.

## LOS OLIVOS

Blink and you might miss it, but the single street that makes up this too-cute town is pretty much the center of Santa Barbara wine country. It might be small but it has several tasting rooms (including Daniel Gehrs and Longoria) and a number of good restaurants. Stop by the **Los Olivos Wine Merchant & Café** (*2879 Grand Ave., Los Olivos, 888-946-3748; www.losolivoscafe.com*) for pizzas, salads and the homemade olive tampenade to start. They also carry more than 150 wines, making it an obvious stop on your tasting tour. Craving a warm and crusty Panini? **Panino** (*2900 Grand Ave., 805-688-9304*) has more than 30 options.

SAN YSIDRO RANCH

### Melville Vineyards & Winery

*5185 East Hwy. 246, Lompoc, 805-735-7030; www.melvillewinery.com*
Built to resemble a Mediterranean villa with lavender filling the grounds, this winery produces chardonnay, viognier, pinot noir and syrah. But this is the Santa Rita Hills, where pinot noir is king and this is definitely one of the places to taste it. It's what brought Ron Melville to the area from Sonoma, and the earthy, densely textured, berry-tinged wine is proof that he made the right move.
Daily 11 a.m.-4 p.m.

## STAY

### ★★★★Bacara Resort & Spa

*8301 Hollister Ave., Santa Barbara, 805-968-0100, 877-422-4245;*
*www.bacararesort.com*
It's a bit out of the way, but a stay at this gorgeous resort delivers a spectacular setting overlooking the Pacific, with a dash of old-time Hollywood glamour in the mix. Three infinity pools are ringed with private, tented cabanas; the spa knows how to take care of the ladies, and the service will make anyone feel like a celeb. It's also a nice place to break from wine tasting, get in a game of tennis, or practice yoga or meditation.
360 rooms. Three restaurants, bars. Children's activity center. Fitness center. Spa. Pool. Golf. Tennis. Business center. Pets accepted. $$$$

### ★★★★Four Seasons Resort The Biltmore Santa Barbara

*1260 Channel Drive, Santa Barbara, 805-969-2261;*
*www.fourseasons.com/santabarbara*
Recently renovated by Beanie Babies owner Ty Warner, this super-luxurious property on 20 lush acres on the Pacific Ocean pays tribute to the region's Spanish colonial history with its red-tiled roof, arches and hacienda-style main building. The guest rooms, located both in the main building and in separate cottages, feature a relaxed Spanish-colonial décor and include down pillows and plush bathrobes. Crisp, white cabanas line the sparkling pool. Besides offering a full menu of massages, facials and body wraps, the spa incorporates botanicals from the gardens into its treatments. After a

CENTRAL COAST

day on back roads squinting to find wineries, an evening at the oceanfront Bella Vista restaurant is just the ticket, particularly if you get a table close to one of the outdoor firepits.
207 rooms. High-speed Internet access. Two restaurants, bar. Spa. Pool. Tennis. Business center. Pets accepted. $$$$

### ★★★★ San Ysidro Ranch, A Rosewood Resort
*900 San Ysidro Lane, Montecito, 805-969-5046, 800-368-6788; www.sanysidroranch.com*
Settle in at this 550-acre paradise and you'll see why John and Jackie Kennedy spent part of their honeymoon here, at this resort tucked away in the foothills of Montecito. Lushly planted acres are filled with fragrant flowers and plants, and stunning vistas of the Pacific Ocean and the Channel Islands can be seen in the distance. The bungalows, with their cozy blend of overstuffed chintz armchairs, oriental rugs and vaulted, wood-clad ceilings, provide luxuries like wood-burning fireplaces and specialty linens. Exceptional cuisine is a hallmark of the property, and the two restaurants

*Bacara Resort & Spa • Four Seasons Resort The Biltmore Santa Barbara • The Canary Hotel • San Ysidro Ranch, A Rosewood Resort*

here provide charming settings for the imaginative food.
41 rooms. Wireless Internet access. Two restaurants, two bars. Fitness center. Pool. Tennis. Pets accepted. $$$$

### Canary Hotel
*31 W. Carillo St., Santa Barbara, 805-884-0300; www.canarysantabarbara.com*
This delightful hotel is what you might imagine your perfect seaside cottage to look like: tall, four-poster beds with crisp, white sheets in front of a huge plasma TV, dark-stained wood floors, beautiful Spanish tile in the bath, and lots of homey touches strewn about—a pair of binoculars casually resting on a stack of books, pretty silver dishes, white candles in large glass hurricanes, a yoga mat in the closet, an iPod dock alarm clock. You may return home and decorate your own bedroom the same way. Restaurants and shopping are within walking distance, and the rooftop deck is the place to catch a cocktail before you crash in your relaxing digs.
97 rooms. Wireless Internet access. Pool. $$$

BACARA RESORT

THE HUNGRY CAT

# EAT

### ★★★Bouchon
*9 W. Victoria St., Santa Barbara, 805-730-1160; www.bouchonsantabarbara.com*
This French-Californian restaurant prides itself on using the freshest local ingredients available, including fish from the Santa Barbara Channel, produce from the surrounding countryside, meats and poultry from local micro-ranches and wine from the Santa Ynez Valley. Order the pan-seared scallops with herb risotto, or try bourbon and maple-glazed duck. The "Molten Lava" chocolate cake is a sweet ending to any meal.
French-Californian menu. Dinner. Reservations recommended. $$$

### ★★★Downey's
*1305 State St., Santa Barbara, 805-966-5006; www.downeyssb.com*
The menu at Downey's, which changes constantly, offers appetizers such as the Santa Barbara mussels with sweet corn and a chili vinaigrette, or homemade duck sausage with lentils. Signature entrées include grilled lamb loin or local sea bass with a ragout of prawns and spring vegetables. The relaxed setting combines to make the place a local favorite.
Continental menu. Dinner. Closed Monday. Reservations recommended. $$$

### ★★★★Miró
*8301 Hollister Ave., Santa Barbara, 805-571-4204, 877-422-4245; www.bacararesort.com*
Santa Barbara's luxurious Bacara Resort is home to the swank Miró Restaurant. Joan Miró-style artwork, deep red dining chairs, a contemporary carpet and fantastic views of the Pacific Ocean set the scene, while the chef creates masterful renditions of traditional Spanish cooking such as oak-grilled lamb chops with aged sherry and pan-roasted lobster with oven-roasted tomatoes. The 12,000-bottle wine cellar has something to match every meal. For a more casual alternative, the Miró Bar and Lounge features homemade sangria and tasty tapas.
Basque, Catalonian menu. Dinner. Closed Mondays. Bar. Business casual attire. Reservations recommended. Valet parking. Outdoor seating. $$$$

CENTRAL COAST

### D'Angelo Bread
*25 W. Gutierrez St., 805-962-5466*
D'Angelo's is the place to go in town for breakfast. Wonderful breads and pastries are available, as well as a wide variety of breakfast dishes made with these delectable products, such as the Eggs Rose (poached eggs on kalamata olive bread with an artichoke spread) and Bananas Foster French Toast. What more could you ask for? Except, perhaps, a foamy latte on the side.
Bakery menu. Breakfast, lunch. Casual attire. $

### Hungry Cat
*1134 Chapala St., Santa Barbara, 805-884-4701;*
*www.thehungrycat.com*
It's small, it's cramped and they don't take reservations, but that doesn't stop locals from coming to this restaurant once, twice, or even three times a week. After a glance at the seafood menu (peel n' eat shrimp, Maine lobster, oysters), you might think the place belongs on the East Coast, but it's actually the Santa Barbara outpost of a popular Hollywood restaurant. Don't care for seafood? The Pug Burger, with bacon, avocado, blue cheese and onion rings, will make you happy to go along. There's also a tasty noodle dish with pancetta and morels. For seafood lovers, the huge platters are the ticket. They serve an "afternoon snack" between 3 p.m. and 5 p.m. on weekends, as well as brunch.
California menu. Brunch, late lunch, dinner. No reservations. $$$

### La Super-Rica Taqueria
*622 N. Milpas St., Santa Barbara, 805-963-4940*
Don't let the funky, rundown shack-like exterior deter you from sampling Santa Barbara's most famous authentic Mexican food, a one-time favorite of gourmet Julia Child. The lines are endless but the fresh tamales and cheap tacos—handmade corn tortillas filled with carne asada, marinated pork, chicken, occasionally Dover sole and more—are beyond delicious and well worth the wait.
Mexican menu. Lunch, dinner. Closed Wenesday. Casual attrire. Cash only. $

### Olio e Limone
*11 West Victoria St., Santa Barbara, 805-899-2699; www.olioelimone.com*
Another favorite of once-local Julia Child, this upscale yet low-key restaurant is the place where both locals and out-of-towners go for the best Italian in the area. Signature dishes include the spaghetti alla bottarga, duck breast, panna cotta and pear carpaccio.
Italian menu. Lunch, dinner. Reservations recommended. $$

### Santa Barbara Shellfish Company
*230 Stearns Wharf, Santa Barbara, 805-966-6676; www.sbfishhouse.com*
If you head to historic Stearns Wharf, be sure to walk all the way to the very end of the pier or you'll miss this great fish shack. Grab a stool at the small bar inside and order up the best of Santa Barbara clam chowder, fresh oysters and mussels, or the whole shebang in the Cioppino: mussels, clams, shrimp, crab and scallops all steaming in a giant bread bowl.
Seafood menu. Lunch, dinner. Outdoor seating. $

## SPA
### ★★★★Bacara Spa
*8301 Hollister Ave., Santa Barbara, 805-968-0100, 877-422-4245;*
*www.bacararesort.com*

MISSION SANTA BARBARA

A saline-filled pool and secluded nooks for sunbathing flank more than 30 treatment rooms and indoor and outdoor massage stations at this heavenly spa. You'll find a variety of traditional treatments here, as well as an Eastern menu that offers Thai massage, reflexology and shiatsu. Ayurvedic treatments include the Shirodhara with Tibetan foot treatment, in which a technician pours warm oil on your forehead (or "third eye"), gives you a scalp massage and applies a warm thermal foot wrap. You'll feel more Zen from head to toe. The rugged terrain of the Santa Ynez Mountains is the perfect place for a rigorous walk, run or hike. Clay tennis courts, pools almost too pretty to swim in and yoga on the beach are just a few of the other fitness options.

### ★★★★Spa at Four Seasons Resort The Biltmore Santa Barbara
*1260 Channel Drive, Santa Barbara, 805-969-2261, 800-819-5053; www.fourseasons.com/santabarbara*

Pure luxury sums up the look and feel of this oceanfront spa, whose design echoes the Spanish colonial style of the Four Seasons Resort in which it's located. Treatment rooms are more residential than spa-like, with kiva fireplaces, plush treatment tables and mission-style furniture. Since you're in wine country, you must try one of the vino-centric treatments. The Vineyard Harvest has you soaking in grapeseed, jasmine, rose and red wine—all of which are full of antioxidants that supposedly help your skin (it can't hurt). A chardonnay clay wrap is then used to remove toxins, followed by a massage. And why not drink the stuff at the same time? A cheese plate and a glass of local wine come along with the treatment. Now that's what we call super-relaxing.

## SEE AND DO
### East Beach
Sun worshippers will love this picturesque stretch of sand located on East Cabrillo Boulevard. Amenities include a full beach house, a snack bar, volleyball courts, a play area for children and bike/rollerblading paths. It also hosts the Santa Barbara Arts and Crafts Show on Sundays.

## El Paseo de Santa Barbara
*812 State St.*
Pick up a few stylin' souvenirs while you're away. Built in the 1920's, this block of galleries, restaurants, and clothing and gift shops is considered the oldest shopping center in California, and a Santa Barbara landmark.

## Market Forays with Laurence Hauben
*805-259-7229; www.marketforays.com*
For a foodie exploration of Santa Barbara, take an all-day cooking class with Laurence Hauben, the leader of Santa Barbara's Slow Food movement. Start your day picking fresh seafood right off the boat; select the freshest and most fragrant fruits and vegetables from neighboring farms (sometimes right off the tree or vine); and then head to an artisanal cheese store before settling into a lovely kitchen to prepare dinner. Finish the day by enjoying your five-course meal, while learning all about the local wine pairings that match. Fees vary.

## Mission Santa Barbara
*2201 Laguna St., Santa Barbara, 805-682-4149; www.sbmission.org*
This unofficial city landmark was built in 1786 as the 10th California mission to be founded by the Spanish Franciscans. A climb to the top of the mission's two towers provides a breathtaking view of Santa Barbara. Self-guided tours operate from 9 a.m. to 5 p.m.

## Stearns Wharf and Ty Warner Sea Center
*State Street and the Pacific Ocean, 805-962-2526; www.sternswharf.org, www.sbnature.org/seacenter*
Once a major shipping hub for all of Southern California, this pier, built in 1872, has dramatic views of Santa Barbara, and is now home to several fresh seafood restaurants, including the delicious Santa Barbara Shellfish Company, and gift shops. The Ty Warner Sea Center, part of the Santa Barbara Museum of Natural History, is an interactive marine education facility where you can pretend you're a scientist for the day, studying animal behavior, looking at microscopic marine life and running tests on ocean water. Daily 10 a.m.-5 p.m.

# CHAPTER 4
# OREGON WINE COUNTRY

*St. Honoré Boulangerie ▪ Domaine Drouhin Vineyard ▪ Andina Restaurant ▪ St. Honoré Boulangerie*

Mother Nature often smiles upon this quiet corner of the country. Because Oregon's mild and rainy climate lends itself to the growing of too many good things to name—naturally abundant fir and pine trees, vegetables, berries, grapes and hops (this is beer-making country, too)—it's no wonder that this is such a green state. The literal and figurative meanings of state go hand in hand when there's so much to protect.

Wine making in Oregon is a relatively recent phenomenon, and all the more impressive given the quality of the wines currently produced here. A group of enologists from the University of California, Davis first had visions in the 1960s of Oregon as prime pinot country, thanks to its climate and topographic features. Today, Oregon is recognized as a world-class wine state, with 15 approved wine-growing regions and 370 wineries producing 72 varieties.
If Yamhill County in the Willamette Valley is the heart of Oregon wine country, pinot noir is the blood. With nearly three times the number of vineyards as other parts of the state, growing more than 10 times as much pinot noir, this is the place to spend your time. From Portland, you can be in a tasting room in a mere 20 minutes. Like other attractions in Oregon, the wine and their makers are exquisite without any of the pretense you'll find elsewhere. And though the Willamette Valley may not have all the epicurean stops

OREGON WINE COUNTRY

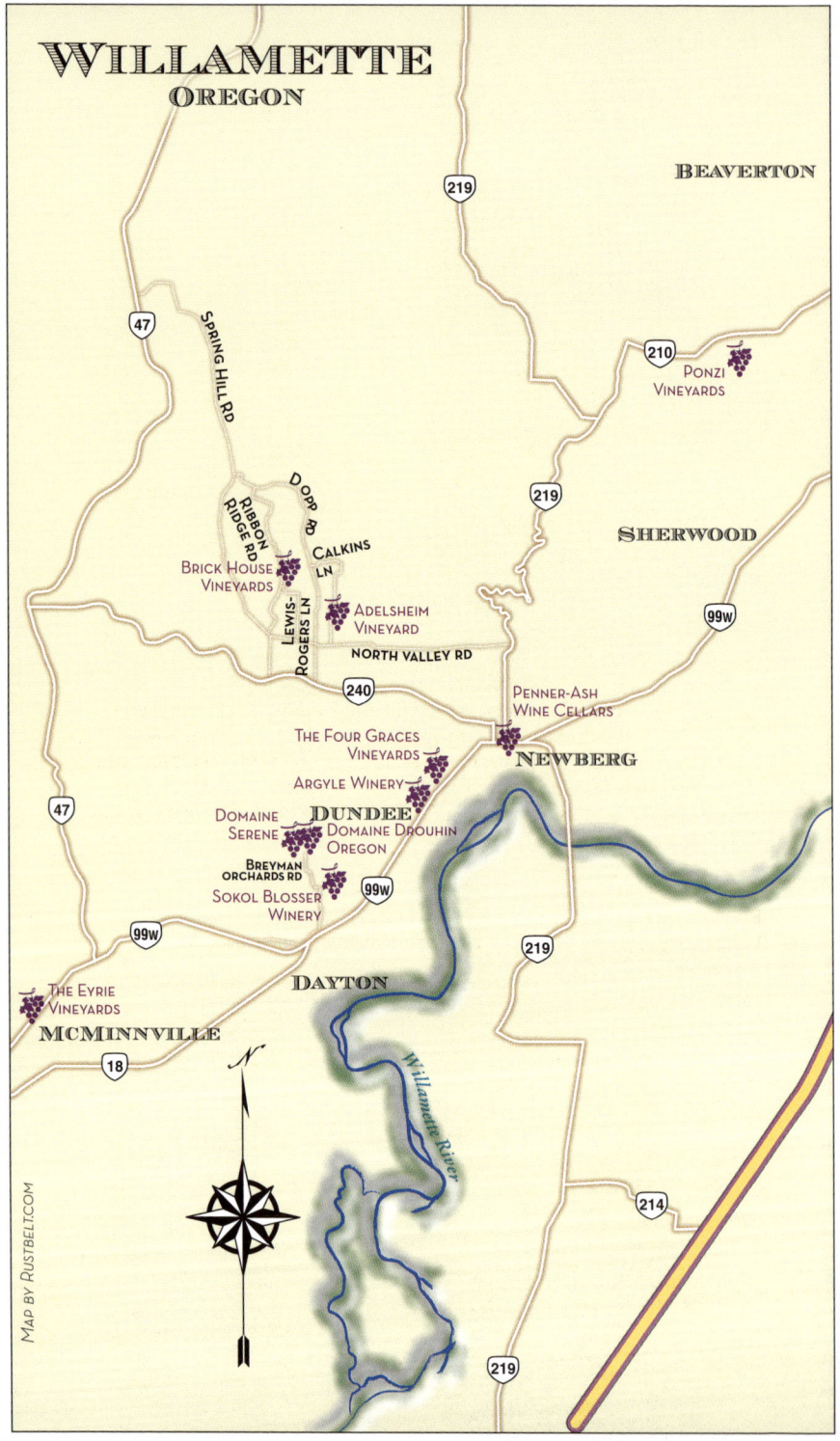

DOMAINE DOUHAIN OREGON

that Napa and Sonoma do, Portland—truly a gastronome's paradise—is just a short drive away, and should be where all Oregon wine trips begin and end.

## WHAT TO SEE

### Adelsheim Vineyard
*16800 N.E. Calkins Lane, Newberg, 503-538-3652; www.adelsheim.com*
Two of Oregon's pinot pioneers, David and Ginny Adelsheim began planting their original 15-acre Willamette Valley vineyard in 1972. More than 35 years later, the estate includes nine vineyards and 168 acres, and produces nearly 50,000 cases of wine annually. Entrenched in the Willamette Valley pinot tradition, Adelsheim was one of the wineries where Véronique Drouhin studied up on Oregon winemaking as an intern for the 1986 vintage, before beginning her family's stateside business in earnest (see Domaine Drouhin Oregon). Today, Adelsheim's grounds in the rolling Chehalem Mountains include a charming tasting room and patio.
Wednesday–Sunday 11 a.m.–4 p.m. Informational tours available.

### Argyle Winery
*691 Highway 99W, Dundee, 503-538-8520, 888-427-4953; www.argylewinery.com*
Located front and center on the main drag in Dundee, Argyle Winery has an elegant tasting room tucked inside a Victorian house that was once the town's city hall. Here, you can taste Argyle's respected pinot noirs and sparkling wines around the long bar or lounge on the wraparound front porch. Rumor has it you may also encounter a ghost, whose presence inspired the name of Argyle's Spirithouse Pinot Noir. Ask the tasting room staff for the full story over your flight of wines.
Daily 11 a.m.–5 p.m. Reservations recommended for groups of 10 or more.

### Brick House Vineyards
*18200 Lewis Rogers Lane, Newberg, 503-538-5136; www.brickhousewines.com*
Almost 20 years ago, Brick House owner Doug Tunnell, a former CBS News international correspondent, decided to return to his Oregon home and

SOKOL BLOSSER

launch a vineyard. The result was a venture that produces fine varietals traditionally from Burgundy: pinot noir, chardonnay and gamay noir. As one of only a handful of certified organic wineries in the Willamette Valley, Brick House wines are grown using traditional methods, without fertilizers or pest control sprays. Even the trellis posts must fit within USDA guidelines—yet Brick House manages to bottle pinots that will proudly stand up to any other chemically-enhanced glass around.

Daily Memorial Day–Thanksgiving. By appointment only the rest of the year.

### Domaine Drouhin Oregon
*6750 Breyman Orchards Road, Dayton, 503-864-2700; www.domainedrouhin.com*

In a barely-40-year-old wine region, the Drouhin family's 128 years of experience and Burgundian winemaking roots certainly gives them the edge in authenticity. Third-generation winemaker Robert Drouhin established Domaine Drouhin in 1987 in the Dundee Hills. His daughter, Véronique, who holds a degree in enology, later assumed responsibility for the family's new world label. Her first vintage was the highly celebrated 1991 release, and her subsequent pinot noirs have continued to garner regular raves from the press and connoisseurs.

Wednesday–Sunday 11 a.m.–4 p.m. Informational tours including tasting and cheese available with reservation.

### Domaine Serene
*6555 N.E. Hilltop Lane, Dayton, 503-864-4600; www.domaineserene.com*

This wine born in Yamhill County's Red Hills has beaten top wines from Burgundy, California and Oregon in blind tastings. Perhaps Domaine Serene owes its worldwide critical acclaim to its founders' vigilance. The focus here is on achieving the best wines using environmentally friendly farming practices—always done with human hands—and low crop yields. The resulting pinot noirs and chardonnays have consistently proven to be concentrated award-winners. With longtime winemaker Tony Rynders departing the vineyard in the spring of 2008, the winery may undergo some hiccups in transition, but we have faith that owners Ken and Grace Even-

# OREGON

stad will continue to uphold the high standards they set when they founded the winery back in 1989.

Wednesday–Monday 11 a.m.–4 p.m. Tours available by appointment. Reservations recommended for groups of 10 or more.

### The Eyrie Vineyards
*935 N.E. 10th Ave., McMinnville, 503-472-6315, 888-440-4970; www.eyrievineyards.com*

If we're going to talk about wine in the Willamette Valley, we should start with Eyrie (prounounced EYE-ree). Founders David and Diana Lett are the Oregon wine industry's first family. Nicknamed "Papa Pinot", David Lett, a young, enthusiastic recent grad at the time, and his family moved to the Willamette Valley in 1966 to test his theory that Burgundian varietals could thrive in the Oregon climate. His success speaks for itself. Lett was the first to plant pinot noir, chardonnay and other grapes in the Willamette Valley and the first to plant pinot gris this side of the Atlantic. He partnered with the other early groundbreakers in Oregon wine—Adelsheim, Erath, Ponzi, and

*Portland & Mount Hood • Suite at Avalon • Portland • Tea at the Heathman Restaurant*

Sokol Blosser—sharing clippings and joining forces to persevere in spite of the lack of recognition they received throughout the '70s. The Eyrie tasting room and winery in McMinnville are separate from the vineyards, but worth a stop to taste the original pinot that set the bar for the rest of the valley.

Wednesday–Sunday 12–5 p.m. Reservations recommended for groups of 8 or more.

### The Four Graces Vineyards
*9605 N.E. Fox Farm Road, Dundee, 800-245-2950; www.thefourgraces.com*

As one of the new kids on the block, this intimate, five-year-old winery is doing something right. The stop, right between Newberg and Dundee, will feel more like a respite in Grandma's kitchen than another tasting room along the wine trail. The hospitality is quaintly old-fashioned, too. In fact, the caterers—yes, there's food included with your flights—dog-sat for us while we sipped, letting us focus on the light, crisp flavors of some of Oregon's best pinot gris. If you like whites, don't miss these. The pinot noirs are worth more than a couple of swirls as well. And the quaint ambience here challenges the pretense of winemaking tradition.

Daily 10 a.m.–5 p.m.

SOKOL BLOSSER

DOMAINE DROUHIN

### Penner-Ash Wine Cellars
*15771 N.E. Ribbon Ridge Road, Newberg, 503-554-5545; www.pennerash.com*
This young Willamette Valley winery has come a long way in less than a decade. Winemaker Lynn Penner-Ash left her post at the helm of Rex Hill (not far down the Valley from her new digs) in 2002. Since then, the label has grown from its first 125 cases of pinot produced in 1998 to the more than 8,000 cases of pinot noir and syrah churned out of its new state-of-the-art facility. The multi-level, gravity-flow winery (practically an industry standard now) was designed to allow nature to do a lot of the physical labor for the employees, as well as to eliminate the damage that comes from pumping wine from one processing stage to another—further refining Penner-Ash's already clearly demonstrated command of pinot.
Thursday–Sunday 11 a.m.–5 p.m. Tours available by appointment.

### Ponzi Vineyards
*14665 S.W. Winery Lane, Beaverton, 503-628-1227; www.ponziwines.com*
Just minutes outside of suburbia and down a narrow road with a broad, pastoral landscape lies a pioneer on the early Oregon wine frontier, Ponzi Vineyards. Established in 1970, the winery was responsible for planting some of the first pinots in Oregon. But pinot isn't the only risk that Dick and Nancy Ponzi have taken; they also were at the forefront of another booming Oregon beverage industry—beer. They founded Oregon's first microbrewery, BridgePort Brewing Company, in 1984 and all the while were accruing critical acclaim for their wines. The Ponzis opened a wine bar in Dundee in 1998, and the Dundee Bistro in 1999, hoping to cultivate the region's culinary scene and promote local Willamette Valley foods. Today the winery, headed by daughter Luisa, includes a wine bar and bistro.
Daily 11 a.m.–5 p.m. Tours available by appointment for groups of five or more.

### Sokol Blosser
*5000 N.E. Sokol Blosser Lane, Dundee, 503-864-2282, 800-582-6668; www.sokolblosser.com*
Part of the small club of early pinot pioneers in Oregon, Bill Blosser and Susan Sokol Blosser

planted their first vines in 1971. Underscoring earth-friendly practices in recent years, Sokol Blosser has been leading the way toward more sustainable winemaking in the Willamette Valley. In 2002, the winery built a cellar certified as Leadership in Energy and Environmental Design (LEED) by the U.S. Green Building Council, and began using organic farming practices on its 80 acres. Three years later, it received the USDA's stamp of approval as a certified organic winery. The latest move toward sustainability was cemented with the handing over of the winery reins in 2008 to Bill and Susan's children, Alex and Alison Sokol Blosser. Pick up a few bottles of the acclaimed Evolution, a delicious white blend that's just right for picnic lunches.

Daily 10 a.m.–4 p.m. Tours Friday–Sunday at 11:30 a.m. and 2:30 p.m. Tour reservations recommended for groups of 8 or more.

## TO DRIVE OR NOT TO DRIVE

There's an inherent problem with wine tasting: you'll need to leave the drive home to someone else. Should no one in your group be willing to volunteer to be the designated driver, here are a few for hire.

**Eco Tours of Oregon** (503-245-1428, 888-868-7733; www.ecotours-of-oregon.com) offers day trips from Portland to wine country that include step-by-step winemaking tours, four or more tasting stops along the way and a picnic spot or restaurant for lunch. **Grape Escape Winery Tours** (503-203-3380; www.grapeescapetours.com) also provides private tours around wine country for small or large groups. **My Chauffeur Wine Tours** (503-969-4370, 877-692-4283; winetouroregon.com) offers four-, six- or eight-hour personalized wine-tasting trips. **Oregon Wine Tours** (503-681-9463; www.orwinetours.com) will design a tour for you or take you wherever you wish if you have your own agenda in mind. **Premiere Tours** (503-244-4653; www.premierewinetours.com) provides customized excursions to Oregon's wine country based on your needs. **Willamette Tours** (360-904-1402, 877-868-7295; www.willamettetours.com) offers five-hour day trips to Willamette Valley wineries. A deli lunch, photography services and a variety of vehicles are also available. **Entourage International Limousines** (866-861-8738; www.TourOregonWines.com) and **Executive Limousine Company** (503-992-8481; www.executivelimocompany.com) have limos and drivers for hire.

# ONE-DAY WINE-TASTING ITINERARY

**EAT:** An early weekend brunch at **Meriwether's** (*2601 N.W. Vaughn St., Portland, 503-228-1250; www.meriwethersnw.com*) delivers an elegant start to a day of indulgence, whether you choose the smoked salmon hash or pancakes made with local blueberries. The restaurant showcases fresh ingredients, with many of them grown on their own farm in Portland's west hills.

**PICK UP:** Made-to-order sandwiches on fresh-baked brown bread or crusty baguettes at **Ken's Artisan Bakery** (*338 N.W. 21st Ave., Portland, 503-248-2202; www.kensartisan.com*) paired with some cheeses and fruits from Trader Joe's across the street make for a tasty afternoon picnic lunch.

**DRIVE:** Head south on I-5 from Portland toward wine country, about a 30-minute drive.

**FIRST STOP:** Take exit 292 and turn right onto Highway 217. Take the Scholls Ferry exit onto Scholls Ferry Road and turn left onto Vandermost Road, following the signs to **Ponzi Vineyards** (see pg. 80). Located just barely outside of Portland's suburbs, this is the closest stop to the city and one of the most historic vineyards.

**SECOND STOP**: Take a left on Scholls Ferry Road and bear left at the first big intersection, staying on Scholls Ferry/Highway 219. The road will wind through gently rolling hills punctuated with red barns, horses and crops, and then open up on top of the Chehalem Mountains to big views of the valley and the heart of Oregon wine country. Turn right on North Valley Road and take another right at NE Calkins Lane. **Adelsheim Vineyard** (see pg. 77) will be on your right.

**EAT:** Spread out your picnic lunch on one of Adelsheim's patio tables overlooking the vineyard.

**THIRD STOP:** Hop back in the car and turn right on North Valley Road, and then left on Ribbon Ridge Road for the quick trip to **Penner-Ash Wine Cellars** (see pg. 80).

**FOURTH STOP:** Take a left and continue south on Ribbon Ridge Road to Highway 240. There, take a right, and then make another right onto Laughlin Road, following signs to **Willakenzie Estate** (*19143 N.E. Laughlin Road, 503-662-3280; www.willakenzie.com*). Set atop a hill overlooking endless vineyards, this is a nice place to wind down.

**DRIVE:** Head back to Portland on Highway 240, passing through Newberg to 99W, followed by I-5N.

**EAT:** Such a day of edible delights should end on a high note. **Le Pigeon** (see pg. 87) will challenge your gourmandizing intrepidity with such creations as foie gras profiteroles and cornbread, bacon and maple ice cream—and those are just the desserts. We don't think you'll be disappointed by any of the bistro masterpieces (skate wing with fresh beans and arugula) chef Gabriel Rucker so lovingly prepares, either.

HEATHMAN HOTEL

## STAY

### ★★★Avalon Hotel
*0455 S.W. Hamilton Court, Portland, 503-802-5800;*
*www.avalonhotelandspa.com*
This peaceful hotel is located on the Willamette River in a quiet section of town and offers a tranquil retreat enhanced by luxurious amenities. In the inviting, fire-warmed two-story lobby, Asian influences blend seamlessly into the contemporary Pacific Northwest design. Standard rooms feature marble baths, plush bathrobes, CD players, cordless phones and private balconies; suites also include fireplaces and double vanities. The excellent Avalon Fitness Club offers cutting-edge classes like Pilates, kickboxing and yoga, in addition to free weights and cardio equipment, with personal trainers on duty to customize workouts.
99 rooms. Wireless Internet access. Complimentary continental breakfast. Restaurant, bar. Spa. $$

### ★★★Heathman Hotel
*1001 S.W. Broadway, Portland, 503-241-4100; www.heathmanhotel.com*
Steps away from downtown Portland's cultural attractions such as the Arlene Schnitzer Concert Hall, Portland Art Museum and Oregon Historical Society Museum, the Heathman dependably garners high praise. It's not hard to see why. With Art Deco mirrors in the Marble Bar, 18th-century French canvases in the historic Tea Court and silk screens by Andy Warhol in the lauded Heathman Restaurant, it's a uniquely appointed space with luxurious amenities to complement the setting. The sleep menu offers a choice of Tempur-Pedic, pillow-top or feather-top beds. Once that's decided, settle into a room that includes Peet's French press coffee, L'Occitane soaps and twice-daily maid service. There's also a film library, afternoon tea and nightly jazz in the Tea Court.
150 rooms. High-speed Internet access. Restaurant, bar. Airport transportation available. Fitness center. Pets accepted. $$

## TWO-DAY WINE-TASTING ITINERARY

Follow the itinerary from page 72 through the fourth stop, and continue as follows.

**DRIVE:** Take Highway 240 to Newberg, turning right onto Highway 99W.

**FIFTH STOP:** If you're up for another low-key tasting before dinner, stop at **The Four Graces Vineyards** (see pg. 79), located just off 99W, before you reach Dundee.

**EAT:** As you're entering Dundee off 99W, you'll find the **Dundee Bistro & Wine Bar** (*100-A S.W. Seventh St., Dundee, 503-554-1650; www.dundeebistro.com*) on your right. Owned by the Ponzi family, this establishment is one of the Willamette Valley's first forays into the restaurant world. The concept pairs nicely with the Ponzi Pinot, and the pizzas are a can't-fail choice here.

**SLEEP:** Take a right on SW Seventh Street, a left on SW View Crest Drive and a right on Ninth Street. Then continue on NE Worden Hill Road. The newly built, elegant **Black Walnut Inn** (*9600 NE Worden Hill Road, Dundee, 866-429-4114; www.blackwalnut-inn.com*) resembles a Tuscan villa set among the hills of Italy. This luxurious bed and breakfast will make you feel at home in the Willamette Valley, delivering super-soft, plush beds and a complimentary gourmet breakfast.

**FIRST STOP:** Head back to 99W and take a right. Then turn right again at NE Sokol Blosser Lane. With one of the earliest tasting room opening times in the area (10 a.m.), **Sokol Blosser** (see pg. 81) makes an easy first stop.

**SECOND STOP:** Continue West on N.E. Sokol Blosser Lane to N.E. Breyman Orchards Road and turn right. Just down the road you'll find **Domaine Drouhin Oregon** (see pg. 78).

**EAT:** Drive back to 99W and turn right, and then left onto the Southeast Dayton Bypass, keeping your eyes peeled for the Salmon River Spur exit. Bear left on N.E. Third Street and stop for lunch at **Bistro Maison** (*729 N.E. Third St., McMinnville, 503-474-1888; www.bistromaison.com*). In case you haven't had enough vino, this French eatery serves up a nice coq au vin.

**THIRD STOP:** Take 18W to 99W south to Bethel Road and take a left. Turn left again at Spring Valley Road for **Cristom Vineyards** (*6905 Spring Valley Road N.W., Salem, 503-375-3068; www.cristomwines.com*), another critically acclaimed pinot producer.

**CONTINUED ON PAGE 76**

OREGON

### ★★★Hotel deLuxe
*729 S.W. 15th Ave., Portland, 503-219-2094; www.hoteldeluxeportland.com*
This downtown boutique hotel salutes Hollywood's golden era with elegant, Art Deco-inspired décor highlighting nearly 400 photos from Tinsletown films. Each floor has its own movie-related theme, from Hitchcock to Frank Capra. The newly renovated rooms, decorated in crisp citrus colors and sprinkled with Hollywood Regency-style accents, from chairs to bedside lamps, are equipped with HD flat-panel TVs, iPod docking stations and pillow menus.
130 rooms. Wireless Internet access. Restaurant, bar. Fitness center. Pets accepted. $$

### The Ace Hotel
*1022 S.W. Stark St., Portland, 503-228-2277; www.acehotel.com*
A stay at this unique hotel won't break the bank. Instead, it will deliver stylish and quirky rooms, a helping of local flavor and a taste of luxury. Opened in 2007, the Ace aimed to fill a void in the hotel industry, providing comfort

*Hotel deLuxe • Andina Restaurant • Avalon Hotel • Hotel deLuxe*

and style at a reasonable price for a discerning, creative crowd—think young screenwriters and guitarists. To create a space where this selective set would want to spend its time, the Ace team carefully restored a 1912 hotel between downtown and the Pearl District, retaining the historical character while updating the place to create a design they describe as "warm minimalism." Next, the staff hired a fleet of local artists to leave its mark in the guest rooms, making each one unique and endeavoring to achieve an "elegantly disheveled" look in all of them. Custom-printed Pendleton wool blankets adorn the organic rubber latex beds. Through the lobby, local brewer Stumptown aromatically roasts divine coffee, and Clyde Common, an adjoining restaurant serving local fare, draws crowds late into the night.
79 rooms. Wireless Internet access. Restaurant, bar. $

OREGON

## TWO-DAY WINE-TASTING ITINERARY

**FOURTH STOP:** Head right around the corner to **St. Innocent** (*5657 Zena Road N.W., Salem, 503-378-1526; www.stinnocent. com*) for another taste of the valley's vino. Drive south on Spring Valley Road and turn right at Zena Road N.W.

**FIFTH STOP:** Traveling back toward Portland, take Highway 221 to 99W and stop in **Argyle Winery**'s tasting room (see pg. 77) to end the trip with a bit of bubbly, one of the winery's specialties (the other being pinot, of course).

**DRIVE:** Head back to Portland, taking 99W north to I-5N.

**EAT:** Finish off your tour of Oregon wine country with a meal at one of Portland's best restaurants for regional Pacific Northwest cuisine, **Paley's Place** (see pg. 88). The cozy vibe, impeccable service and flawless food (think ricotta ravioli with peas and truffle butter) is the perfect recipe for a relaxing evening.

## EAT

### ★★★Genoa
*2832 S.E. Belmont St., Portland, 503-238-1464; www.genoarestaurant.com*

Housed in a windowless, unassuming storefront, Genoa is a hidden gem where glorious, old-country-style Italian feasts are served nightly. Control freaks need not bother coming: there is no printed menu at Genoa. Your waiter will offer you a choice of three entrées, but all the other decisions rest in the hands of the chef. The menu is prix fixe, with four- or seven-course options. Dinner at Genoa is a lengthy, leisurely, lovely affair. The service is hospitable and knowledgeable, and nothing is rushed, giving you time to savor your food and your company.

Italian menu. Dinner. Closed Monday. Reservations required. Casual attire. $$$

### Andina
*1314 N.W. Glisan St., Portland, 503-228-9535; www.andinarestaurant.com*

This Peruvian restaurant serves up unique small plates and refreshing cocktails that aim to bring the flavors of Peru to the Pearl District. Dishes include quinoa-crusted diver scallops atop wilted spinach and a pisco-marinated New York strip accompanied by a mojito or caipirinha. Expect fresh, authentic food; everyone here—from the owners to the chef and the cooking staff—is a Peruvian native.

Peruvian menu. Lunch, dinner. Bar. Reservations accepted. $

### Bluehour
*250 N.W. 13th Ave., Portland, 503-226-3394; www.bluehouronline.com*

This is the quintessential Pearl District restaurant. The space is a chic,

revamped warehouse that epitomizes the neighborhood's relatively recent transition from industrial to upscale. And just as you'll find at so many other eateries in this city, the emphasis here is on fresh and local. Bread is baked onsite each morning, all of the sauces and dressings are created daily and even the vanilla ice cream, served with such delights as the rhubarb (local, of course) shortcake, is homemade. At lunch, choose from classics like grilled burgers or cobb salads. For dinner, the choices are slightly more elegant, with house staples like gnocchi with Italian black truffles and fontina val d'Aosta, or bacon-wrapped seared sea scallops.
Mediterranean menu. Lunch, dinner, Sunday brunch. Bar. Reservations accepted, but half of the tables are reserved for walk-ins. Business attire. Outdoor seating. $$

### Le Pigeon
*738 E. Burnside St., Portland,*
*503-546-8796; www.lepigeon.com*
This local favorite is led by 27-year-old chef/owner Gabriel Rucker, who has created an intimate bistro that's perfectly suited for dinner at the end of a day of wine tasting. Grab a seat at the bar and brace yourself to dig into whatever adventurous seasonal creations Rucker has on the menu. From an inspired skate with pork, beans and arugula, to a tamer lamb with cucumber, radicchio and blue cheese, everything is sure to please the palate. And whatever you do, don't skip dessert.
French menu. Dinner. $$

### St. Honoré Boulangerie
*2335 N.W. Thurman St., Portland,*
*503-445-4342;*
*www.sainthonorebakery.com*
With a pain au chocolat that even Francophiles will attest is the genuine article, carefully crafted croque monsieurs and award-winning bread, you'll think you've died and gone to France after a visit to this café. (The staff won't give you any reason to believe you haven't—the service is regularly subpar.) But the folks at this bakery are doing enough right—croissants, éclairs, gateaux, baguettes, you get the picture—to keep this corner café packed at all hours.
French bakery and café. Breakfast, lunch, dinner. $

THE ACE HOTEL

ANDINA

AVALON HOTEL

### Stumptown Coffee Roasters
*4525 S.E. Division St.; 3356 S.E. Belmont St.; 128 S.W. Third Ave.; 1026 SW Stark, 503-230-7797; www.stumptowncofee.com*
No visit to the Pacific Northwest would be complete without some killer joe. You'll find it at Stumptown, Portland's brewer of choice. Each cup of java served at this coffee shop, which has locations throughout the city, is pressed to order. Being selective with beans, painstakingly careful with the roasting process and skilled at the bar makes for perfection. Connoisseurs will appreciate what some call a wine-like approach to the bean.
Coffee menu. $

### Paley's Place
*1204 N.W. 21st Ave., Portland, 503-243-2403; www.paleysplace.net*
If Bluehour typifies the Pearl District, Paley's is the Northwest. Situated about 10 blocks apart, the two neighborhoods have very different vibes. The Paleys behind Paley's Place are New York transplants who take full advantage of the Pacific Northwest's fresh, local ingredients to consistently deliver second-to-none seafood (we especially savored the scallops) and a sous-vide Kobe Sirloin that will ruin subsequent steak dinners for you. The critically acclaimed restaurant is housed in one of Portland's historic Victorian houses, and offers several seating options: a generous front porch, an intimate dining room, a fresh-air patio and a cozy bar area that's perfect for some wine, a bite to eat and friendly conversation.
Seafood menu. Dinner. Bar. Outdoor seating. Reservations recommended. $$

### Pok Pok
*3226 S.E. Division St., Portland, 503-232-1387; www.pokpokpdx.com*
The waits are always long but worth it, at this stylish Portland Thai spot. Locals head to the bar across the street to have a drink while they wait for a table (Pok Pok's hostess will even call the bartender when it's ready). The menu is inspired by Thai street food and comes mostly in the form of small plates to share. The kai yaang, a lemongrass, garlic, pepper and cilantro stuffed game hen served with a spicy sweet and sour dipping sauce, is

the restaurant's signature dish. The namesake dish, the made-to-order pok pok salad is a mélange of green papaya, tomatoes, beans, thai chili, tamarind, fish sauce, garlic, palm sugar, dried shrimp and peanuts mixed in a mortar and pestle, aka pok pok.
Thai menu. Lunch, dinner. Closed Sunday. Bar. Outdoor seating. Reservations accepted only for parties of five or more. $

## SPA

### ★★★Avalon Spa
*0455 S.W. Hamilton Court, Portland, 503-802-5900*
This waterside retreat on the western shore of the Willamette River captures the essence of the Pacific Northwest—witness the Rain Massage ($260, 120 minutes)—while also paying tribute to Asian and European traditions. Wholeheartedly dedicated to well-being, the spa's carefully constructed treatment menu utilizes natural ingredients and innovative therapies to relax all guests. The spa also offers salon services, including hair styling, manicures, pedicures and waxing. But perhaps the best part of this spa is the fitness center, which boasts a calendar chock-full of different classes: yoga, Pilates and even a few offbeat ones, like salsa dancing and a ballet workout.

## SHOP

### The Bee and Thistle
*120 N.W. 10th Ave., Portland, 503-222-3397; www.thebeeandthistle.com*
This unique Pearl District boutique (located just around the corner from an outdoor mall packed with national chain stores including Anthropologie and Lululemon) features finds like locally made jewelry, handbags and accessories. There are also one-of-a-kind frocks and trend-setting shoes.
Daily 11 a.m.–7 p.m.

### Cheeky B
*906 N.W. 14th Ave., Portland, 503-274-0229; www.cheekyboutique.com*
This shop, another locally owned treasure trove showcasing Portland designers, stocks goods for the home, jewelry, handbags, stationary and lots of other one-of-a-kind finds. The attractive letterpress notecard sets make perfect gifts.
Monday–Saturday 10 a.m.–6 p.m., Sunday 11 a.m.–5 p.m.

### Lizard Lounge
*1323 N.W. Irving St., Portland, 503-416-7476; www.lizardloungepdx.com*
More than a store, this unique gathering place lets you sip coffee and browse the web or the racks, which are stocked with laidback, surf-influenced casual clothing. Brands include Billabong, C&C California and Three Dots among others.
Monday–Saturday 10 a.m.–7 p.m.

### Powell's City of Books
*1005 W. Burnside, Portland, 503-228-4651, 800-878-7323; www.powells.com*
This store is an essential stop for anyone even remotely literarily inclined. Encompassing a full city block, Powell's is the largest independent bookseller in the world. The store stocks both new and used books and doesn't segregate the two, making for a brilliant browsing experience.
Daily 9 a.m.–11p.m.

## SEE & DO

Should your visit happen to fall the first or last week of the month and include a Thursday, be sure to set

PORTLAND SKYLINE

aside time to explore Portland's thriving art scene. The first Thursday (*www.firstthursdayportland.com*) of the month, art galleries in the Pearl District extend their hours (generally 6 p.m. to 9 p.m.) and debut their latest openings. Expect a lot of people, tunes and wine. On the last Thursday (*www.artonalberta.org/last_thursday.aspx*) the crowd is on the other side of the Willamette in the Alberta Arts District for a similar—yet very different—gathering from about 5 p.m. to 9:30 p.m. For live local music any night of the month, head to the retro swank **Doug Fir** (*830 E. Burnside, Portland, 503-231-9663; www.dougfirlounge.com*) where there's always some kind of scene.

## TIME IT

Wineries that aren't open any other time of year unlock their doors Memorial and Thanksgiving weekends as they introduce new releases and older vintages. Some wineries host live musicians to enhance the tasting experience. Expect the winemakers themselves to be on hand to greet you personally and help you get to know Oregon wine. For more information, call the Willamette Valley Wineries Association at 503-646-2985.

# CHAPTER 5
# WASHINGTON

*Brian Carter Cellars • The Fairmont Olympic Hotel • Vineyard • Hotel Vintage Park*

Best known for its cafés and once-powerful grunge scene, the Seattle area may soon have to give up its hipster image. Washington has emerged as one of the largest wine regions in the U.S., second only to California, specializing in chardonnay, riesling, merlot, cabernet sauvignon and syrah. Of the state's 400-some wineries, more than 35 are in small-town Woodinville, which sits at the northern end of the Sammamish River Valley and is about 17 miles from downtown Seattle. The vineyards themselves lie in Eastern Washington, not Woodinville, since the western half of the state is, no surprise, too wet and not sunny enough to grow adequate grapes. That's not to say that there isn't much to see and do at the wineries themselves. The oldest winery in the state is in Woodinville, and in addition to the tastings and classes, it hosts summer concerts with musicians like Ringo Starr Plus, events such as the Passport to Woodinville grant access to both established estates and smaller boutique wineries. The area is also host to many fine dining options and cultural outings. So, oenophiles, it's time to put down your Starbucks cup and get on the wine trail.

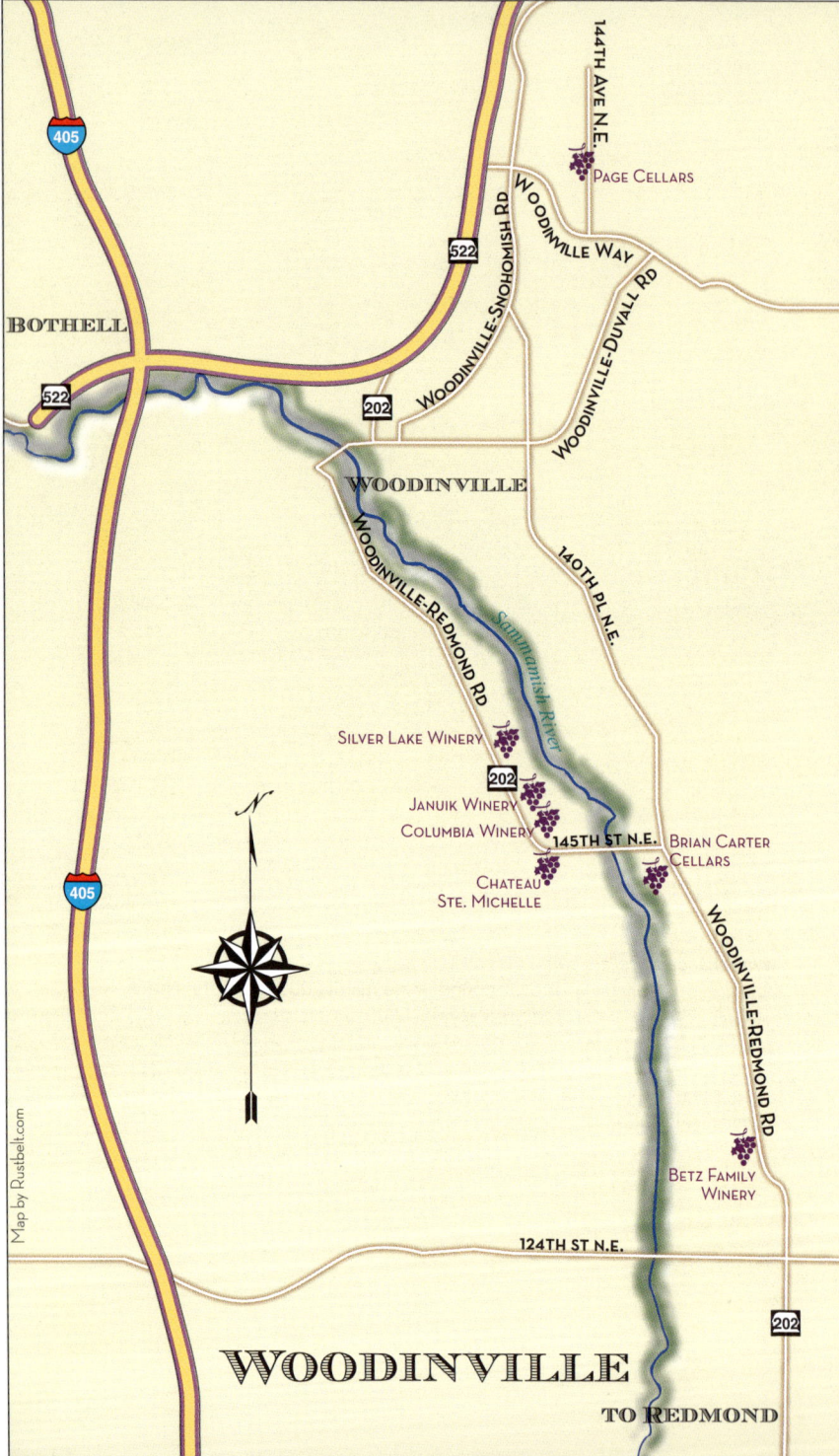

COLUMBIA WINERY

# TASTE

### Betz Family Winery
*13244 Woodinville Redmond Road N.E., Redmond, 425-861-9823; www.betzfamilywinery.com*

If you're a fan of reds, a stop at Betz is a requirement—the winery specializes in the rich, dark purple stuff, particularly bordeaux varietals like cabernet sauvignon and merlot. The patriarch of the family-run business, Bob Betz, is one of only 264 people in the world to hold the title of Master of Wine, and though you won't get much face time with the man (the winery doesn't have a tasting room or tours), try to visit during the Release Weekends in the fall (for Rhone-style wines) and late winter (Bordeaux-style wines). If you can, get your hands on the winery's 2005 Clos de Betz, a coveted vintage that's a blend of merlot, cabernet sauvignon, malbec and cabernet franc. Call for Release Weekend details.

### Brian Carter Cellars
*14419 Woodinville-Redmond Road, Woodinville, 425-806-9463; www.briancartercellars.com*

Brian Carter Cellars will break ground in the fall of 2008 to create a new winery with a heated outdoor courtyard, a private tasting library and a spacious public tasting room, complete with a full kitchen and two tasting bars. The new construction is an indicator of BCC's recent success, but in the meantime, its cozy, small yellow house tasting room offers samples of handcrafted European-style blends. Go there to imbibe on little known local wines. The amiable staff will help you find some good bottles. Monday, Thursday noon-5 p.m., Friday-Sunday noon-6 p.m.

### Chateau Ste. Michelle
*14111 N.E. 145th St., Woodinville, 425-488-1133, 800-267-6793; www.ste-michelle.com*

Although it's the oldest winery in the state, Chateau Ste. Michelle doesn't show any wear and tear. The beautiful, pristine white chateau is surrounded by perfectly manicured grounds, and Ste. Michelle continues to churn out delicious wine. It was among the first in Washington to plant riesling,

THE FAIRMONT OLYMPIC HOTEL

and the winery is still an advocate for the grape, having created the yearly Riesling Rendezvous seminar to celebrate it. But the winery is also known for its chardonnay, merlot and cabernet. If you head over to the chateau, carve out time to browse the well-stocked shop and tasting room. Try to coincide your trip with one of the chateau's big outdoor summer concerts, which have included headliners such as Earth, Wind & Fire; Crosby, Stills & Nash; and B.B. King.
Daily 10 a.m.-5 p.m.

### Columbia Winery
*14030 N.E. 145th St., Woodinville, 425-482-7490, 800-488-2347; www.columbiawinery.com*
Columbia Winery's humble beginnings can be traced back to a garage in the Seattle neighborhood of Laurelhurst. In that garage in 1962, the first bottles were vinted. Founded by 10 friends, the operation has grown steadily over the years. The story goes that while he was a vintner at Columbia, David Lake made the first vineyard-designated wines in the state and was

*Silver Lake Winery • Columbia Winery • Woodinville • Dinner at the Georgian*

the first winemaker in Washington to produce varietals such as syrah, cabernet franc and pinot gris. Naturally, you'll want to sample those wines here. But Columbia's rieslings and gewürztraminers have made names for themselves as well. So make sure you're plenty thirsty when you come, especially since Columbia lays claim to the largest wine-tasting bar in the state.
Daily 10 a.m.-6 p.m.

### Januik Winery
*14710 Woodinville-Redmond Road N.E., Woodinville, 425-481-5502; www.januikwinery.com*
Family-owned Januik is ushering in a new kind of winery. Instead of the rustic, Old World-style estate, Januik's state-of-the-art building is contemporary and sleek. Wood elements and an outdoor fireplace inject warmth into the endless concrete structures, whose linear design mimics rows of vineyards. If you need an extra dose of warmth, visit the tasting room, which Januik shares with the independent Novelty Hill winery, to sip the winery's limited-release bottles. Try Januik's acclaimed chardonnay, merlot,

HOTEL MONACO

SILVER LAKE WINERY

syrah and cabernet sauvignon. You can also take classes and hold private functions on the grounds. Daily 11 a.m.-5 p.m.

### Page Cellars
*19495 144th Ave. N.E., Woodinville,*
*253-232-9463; www.pagecellars.com*
Owners Jim and Rothelle Page are passionate about their reds, as is evident from the 2004 Preface, a cabernet that starts out aromatic and deep, and finishes elegantly, or their 2005 Sauvignon Blanc, a crisp tipple reminiscent of Anjou pears and apples. It doesn't hurt that the winery doesn't shy away from fun names for their wines, such as the 2003 Libra de Carta (i.e., "Paperback Novel") and a syrah called Lick My Lips.
Saturday noon-4 p.m.

### Silver Lake Winery
*15029 Woodinville-Redmond Road, Woodinville,*
*425-485-2437; www.silverlakewinery.com*
A shared love of wine prompted three University of Washington professors and a local real estate investor to start Silver Lake Wines in 1987. Today, more than 1,200 wine enthusiasts are members of Washington's largest consumer-owned winery. Silver Lake uses Bordeaux, Rhone and Burgundian grape varietals from Roza Hills vineyard in Eastern Washington to produce its three collections: cask wines, reserve wines and grand reserve wines. After uncorking a few in the winery's tasting room, try to pop into one of the seminars, covering topics such as "How to Bottle Your Own Wine," "Red Wine & Chocolates" and "Wine Making 101."
Monday-Saturday 11 a.m.-5 p.m.,
Sunday noon-5 p.m.

## STAY

### ★★★★ The Fairmont Olympic Hotel
*411 University St., Seattle, 206-621-1700,*
*800-257-7544; www.fairmont.com/seattle*
The Fairmont Olympic Hotel brings grand tradition and lots of pampering to downtown Seattle, carefully blending its 1920s Italian Renaissance heritage with 21st-century hospitality. The hotel is located in Rainier Square, only minutes from the city's top attractions. The guest rooms and suites are tasteful, homey retreats outfitted with floral draperies and period furnishings. Not that you should

WASHINGTON

## TOURS

### Bon Vivant Wine Tours
*206-437-1298; www.bonvivanttours.com*
Hop on Bon Vivant's white touring van for half-day or full-day tours of Woodinville wineries. If you want a more off-the-beaten-path tour, opt for the one that visits the town's smaller boutique wineries.

### Winery Bus
*425-351-6328; www.winerybus.com*
For those who can't be tied down to a rigid winery itinerary, but need transportation and a designated driver, take the Winery Bus. You can rent a "party bus"—basically a nice bus with a tricked-out interior—for the four-hour Woodinville tour and a driver will shuttle you around to three local wineries of your choice. If you choose the six-hour version, you can hit up four or five wineries.

spend all your time in your room—head to The Georgian restaurant, where the bounty of the Pacific Northwest is the focus with dishes such as the grilled halibut. Traditional high tea service is a treat worth your time. Shuckers is a popular oyster bar where Seattle's famous microbrews are savored, as well as the little shelled wonders prepared any way you want 'em: house-smoked, baked, Rockefeller, pan-fried, barbequed, raw…the list goes on.
450 rooms. Pets accepted, some restrictions. High-speed Internet access. Two restaurants, two bars. Fitness room. Spa. Indoor pool, whirlpool. $$$

### ★★★Hotel Monaco
*1101 Fourth Ave., Seattle, 206-621-1770, 800-715-6513; www.monaco-seattle.com*
This hip hotel is centrally located near the waterfront, Pike Place Market, the Seattle Art Museum and great shopping. The palette of reds, yellows and blues, overhanging wrought iron chandeliers, and cushy furnishings make for an intimate atmosphere. The complimentary evening wine reception in the two-story lobby is the perfect place for guests to relax in front of the fireplace or mingle with others. Quirky hotel activities include complimentary chair massages on Tuesdays and Thursdays, a fortune-teller on Wednesdays and Saturdays, and Guitar Hero jam sessions on Fridays. And quirky turns downright cute with the fact that if you're feeling lonely, you can request a temporary pet goldfish and no one will bat an eye. The Southern-inspired restaurant, Sazerac, serves locally grown produce and California wines.
189 rooms. Wireless Internet access. Restaurant, bar. Pets accepted. $$$

HOTEL VINTAGE PARK

### ★★★Hotel Vintage Park
*1100 Fifth Ave., Seattle, 206-624-8000, 800-853-3914; www.hotelvintagepark.com*
Built in 1926, this beautifully renovated hotel is a homage to Washington wine country. It offers well-appointed and finely furnished (rich fabrics and cherry wood furniture) guest rooms, each named after a local winery or vineyard. It's also in the heart of the city and just steps from shops, theaters and restaurants. If too much sightseeing takes its toll, consider sitting by the fireplace in the cozy lobby and tasting local varietals at the hotel's complimentary nightly reception. After whetting your palate, Tulio Ristorante, the in-house Italian restaurant and local favorite, is the perfect place to grab a bite and more vino.
126 rooms. Wireless Internet access. Restaurant, bar. Pets accepted. $$

### ★★★Inn at the Market
*86 Pine St., Seattle, 206-443-3600, 800-446-4484; www.innatthemarket.com*
Seattle's renowned creative spirit is alive and kicking at the delightful Inn at the Market, thanks to its charming, calming courtyard, which is surrounded by the hotel's artsy boutiques. Picturesque views and cultural attractions are just outside the door at the country-chic home-away-from-home, boasting a prime spot at the vibrant Pike Place Market, and overlooking the waters of Elliott Bay. Accommodations include access to in-room massages and special Tempur-Pedic mattresses for restful sleep. The rooftop garden provides a tranquil place to daydream or keep watch on the goings-on at the market below.
70 rooms. Wireless Internet access. Three restaurants, bar. Pets accepted. $$$

### ★★★Mayflower Park Hotel
*405 Olive Way, Seattle, 206-623-8700, 800-426-5100; www.mayflowerpark.com*
The historic Mayflower Park Hotel offers a killer location in the heart of Seattle, near the monorail, many eclectic shops, and attractions like Pike Place Market and Seattle Center. But even if it weren't in the city's center, this beautiful hotel would still be a destination unto itself. First opened in

1927 as The Bergonian, the Mayflower has since been renovated to recapture the grandeur and classic style of days gone by. Guest rooms are luxurious with beautiful furnishings, rich fabrics, large-screen televisions, fluffy bathrobes and Gilchrist & Soames bath amenities, while everyone—from the concierge to room service staff—provides friendly and gracious service. If you're looking to switch off the vino for a bit, the hotel's bar, Oliver's, consistently comes out on top in Seattle's annual Martini Classic Challenge.
161 rooms. Wireless Internet access. Restaurant, two bars. $$

### ★★★Willows Lodge
*14580 N.E. 145th St., Woodinville, 425-424-3900, 877-424-3930; www.willowslodge.com*
Bordering the Sammamish River in Washington's western wine country, the Willows Lodge is an exceptional getaway. Industrial-chic meets Native American sensibilities at this former hunting lodge, and guests can feel, behind the modernist design, the ambience of the lodge's rustic beginnings. Stained concrete, slate and sleek lines reveal a modern slant in the accommodations, while dynamic artwork crafted by Northwest coast Native Americans showcases local pride. Lush, landscaped gardens complete with a hidden courtyard create a wonderful enclosure for reading and lounging, and the herb and edible plant gardens serve as the inspiration behind the excellent menus at The Herbfarm and Barking Frog restaurants. The resort's sanctuary-like atmosphere is enhanced by a full-service spa that offers a host of soothing and beautifying treatments.
84 rooms. Complimentary continental breakfast. Two restaurants, two bars. Fitness center. Spa. Pets accepted. $$$

## EAT

### ★★★Cafe Flora
*2901 E. Madison St., Seattle, 206-325-9100; www.cafeflora.com*
There are people who believe that the words delicious and innovative could never be used to describe vegetarian cuisine, but Cafe Flora proves them wrong. Since 1991, this Seattle gem has been turning out fresh and nutritious fare that consistently receives raves from vegetarians and carnivores alike. Herbs from the restaurant's own garden are used in seasonal dishes like Yakima Valley polenta with bing cherries soaked in port sauce, and a sauté of local snap peas, pea vines and Walla Walla onions.
Vegetarian menu. Lunch, dinner, brunch. Children's menu. $$

### ★★★Etta's Seafood
*2020 Western Ave., Seattle, 206-443-6000; www.tomdouglas.com*
With an atmosphere as colorful as the food, Etta's brings in droves of hungry patrons both day and night. This casual seafood house is just half a block from the popular Pikes Peak Market and is named after the owners' daughter, Loretta. Its large windows overlook the bustling farmers' market, which supplies a majority of the fresh ingredients on the menu. There's something on the list for everyone, from fish and chips to juicy crab cakes to Oregon country beef burgers.
Seafood menu. Lunch, dinner, brunch. Bar. Children's menu. Casual attire. Reservations recommended. $$$

PURPLE CAFÉ AND WINE BAR

### ★★★★The Georgian
*411 University St., Seattle, 206-621-7889; www.fairmont.com/seattle*
The Fairmont Olympic Hotel in Seattle houses one of the most acclaimed restaurants in the Pacific Northwest. The Georgian's elegant décor features crystal chandeliers, arched ceilings and potted palms. Executive chef Gavin Stephenson brings his culinary expertise to the restaurant after honing his skills at the Savoy Hotel in London and as the personal chef to Saudi Prince Al-Waleed Bin Talal Alsaud. Stephenson is certainly a master of all dishes related to seafood, but he also excels on terra firma with creations such as a salad of organic greens and sprouts with artichokes, spring asparagus and cured tomatoes, filet of Angus beef topped with braised oxtail and shallots, and black and white chocolate soufflé.
American, French, Northwest menu. Breakfast, lunch, dinner. Bar. Children's menu. Business casual attire. Reservations recommended. Valet parking. $$$

### ★★★★The Herbfarm
*14590 N.E. 145th St., Woodinville, 425-485-5300; www.theherbfarm.com*
Chef Keith Luce creates seasonal, themed meals based on the bounty of the restaurant's own gardens and farm, plus produce, meats and artisanal cheeses sourced from local growers, producers, ranchers and fishermen. Surrounded by antiques and candlelight (and often, the music of a pretty good flamenco guitarist), you'll indulge in a four-hour meal of nine courses, paired with five or six complementary wines.
Pacific Northwest menu. Dinner. Closed Monday-Wednesday. Business-casual attire. Reservations recommended. $$$$

### ★★★★Lampreia Restaurant
*2400 First Ave., Seattle, 206-443-3301; www.lampreiarestaurant.com*
Not content with serving typical Italian food, chef Scott Carsberg prepares simple meals that nevertheless continue to astound and challenge the palate. The Tomatoes Lampreia, a dish that showcases up to 10 different preparations of the humble fruit, is a signature. Numerous tableside presentations by the charming service staff add flair to the culinary experience.

International menu. Dinner. Closed Sunday-Monday. Business-casual attire. Reservations recommended. Valet parking. $$$

### Purple Café and Wine Bar
*14459 Woodinville-Redmond Road N.E., Woodinville, 425-483-7129; www.thepurplecafe.com*
For a low-key evening out, head to the Purple Café, which uses fresh, seasonal ingredients to craft its sandwiches, pizzas and pastas. The extensive wine menu devotes a page to Woodinville labels, so head here if you don't have time to check out all the vineyards in the area. Beginner wine lovers will make use of the glossary in the back of the menu to ensure they order the perfect bottle to pair with one of the café's many cheese flights. American menu. Lunch, dinner. Children's menu. Casual attire. Reservations recommended. $$

*Seattle Art Museum • Hoppin' John Fritters at Cafe Flora • Dining Room at The Georgian • Sur LaTable*

## SPA

### Napolitano Day Spa Salon
*614 W. McGraw St., Seattle, 206-282-4343; www.napolitanospa.com*
Walking up to the steps of Napolitano, you may get a whiff of the garden's fragrant lavender, mint and rosemary plants, which are used in the spa's treatments. Tucked inside a lovely turn-of-the-century Victorian house, you'll find a cozy space with hardwood floors, antique furniture and a fireplace. It's so inviting, you may want to stay a while and take a breather from your wine weekend. Treat your dehydrated skin to the Special Care Facial, a renewing vitamin treatment that includes hand and foot acupressure massages with heated mitts. Your feet may still be sore from all the winery tours, so get the Essential Spa Pedicure, which features a sea and mineral salt scrub, callous treatments and heated boots. Afterward, you still won't want to leave the spa, but you won't be able to blame your sore peds anymore.

DIMITRIOU'S JAZZ ALLEY

SEATTLE WATERFRONT

# SHOP

### Alderwood Mall
*3000 184th St. S.W., Lynnwood, 425-771-1211; www.alderwoodmall.com*
The largest shopping center in north Seattle, the Alderwood Mall is an upscale retail and entertainment destination with 175-plus shops in an indoor village and on outdoor terraces. Alderwood is anchored by department stores Nordstrom and Macy's, as well as a 16-screen movie theater. Monday-Thursday 10 a.m.-9:30 p.m., Friday-Saturday 10 a.m-10 p.m., Sunday 11 a.m.-7 p.m.

### Downtown Shopping District
*First Avenue to Seventh Avenue and Madison Street to Pine Street, Seattle; www.downtownseattle.com*
For some prime window-shopping, head to First and Second Avenues, which are lined with fashionable boutiques, upscale galleries and a few curiosities. Fifth and Sixth Avenues brim with jewelry, kitchen and clothing stores ranging from small boutiques to mega-sized versions of national staples. There are also a pair of malls on Pine Street: Westlake (between Fourth and Fifth Avenues), a fairly typical enclosed shopping center, and the ritzy Pacific Place mall, downtown Seattle's newest large, stylish retail destination. The centerpiece of the whole shopping district is **Nordstrom** (*500 Pine St.*), the flagship of the department store chain.

### Sur La Table
*84 Pine St., Seattle, in Pike Place Market, 206-448-2244; www.surlatable.com*
In the 1970s, Seattle spawned this clearinghouse for hard-to-find kitchen gear, and it soon became known as a source for cookware, small appliances, cutlery, kitchen tools, linens, tableware, gadgets and specialty foods. Now a nationwide chain, Sur La Table has since expanded its offerings to include cooking classes, chef demonstrations and cookbook author signings. Cooking connoisseurs will discover such finds as cool oven mitts, zest graters, copper whisks, onion soup bowls and inspired TV dinner trays. Daily.

### University Village Shopping
*45th St. N.E., Seattle, 206-523-0622; www.uvillage.com*
Located near the University of Washington campus

in northeast Seattle, the open-air University Village has a rare balance of national (the ubiquitous Gap) and local establishments (the cutesy Glassybaby). Daily.

## SEE AND DO

### The 5th Avenue Theatre
*1308 Fifth Ave., Seattle, 206-625-1418, 888-584-4849; www.5thavenue.org*
This historic theater, which opened as a vaudeville house in 1926, now features musicals, concerts, films and lectures. Its ornate interior, modeled after some of China's architectural treasures, may well distract you from whatever is taking place onstage.

### ACT Theatre
*700 Union St., Seattle, 206-292-7676; www.acttheatre.org*
ACT Theatre stages contemporary (read: edgy and daring) pieces as well as classic plays and musicals. Performances are held in two main theaters in Kreielsheimer Place, a renovation of the historic Eagles Auditorium completed in 1996. The Allen was carved out of the old auditorium's floor; the top row of seats is actually at ground level. The Falls features a restored Joshua Green Foundation Vault, used by the Eagles as a bank vault. Daily.

### Century Ballroom
*915 E. Pine St., Seattle, 206-324 7263, 206-325-6500 (tickets); www.centuryballroom.com*
Home to one of Seattle's largest dance floors (2,000 square feet of refinished wood), the stylish Century Ballroom is the place to go for swing and salsa dancing in the Emerald City. Many nights are themed (tango night, salsa night, swing night). For those with two left feet, don't worry, lessons are offered. While many are multiweek endeavors, there are occasional one-shot workshops good for out-of-town visitors. With a full bar, seating at comfortable tables and a cavernous downtown location, the venue also hosts a number of concerts every month, mostly jazz and salsa acts. A popular restaurant here serves dinner. The cuisine is classic Pacific Northwest with Asian embellishments. Daily.

### Dimitriou's Jazz Alley
*2033 Sixth Ave., Seattle, 206-441-9729; www.jazzalley.com*
Widely considered the best jazz club in Seattle, this downtown venue originally opened in the University District in 1979, then moved downtown in 1985, and has seen performances by such big names as Taj Mahal and Eartha Kitt. The atmosphere is refined, with chairs and tables surrounding the circular stage, and a mezzanine above. A renovation in 2002 expanded Jazz Alley's capacity and bolstered the sound system while retaining the heralded ambiance. The onsite restaurant serves an international menu with many Italian and Northwestern dishes. Tuesday-Sunday doors open 5:30 p.m.

### Seattle Art Museum
*1300 First Ave., Seattle, 206-625-8900; www.seattleartmuseum.org*
The Seattle Art Museum (known locally as SAM) is the premiere facility of its kind in the Pacific Northwest, and we're not just saying that because its entrance is guarded by an animated, 48-foot-tall sculpture named Hammering Man. There is something for everybody here, from ancient Greek sculpture to 20th-century Russian decorative art. Of particular note are the collections of contemporary art (with pieces

FREMONT OKTOBERFEST

by Andy Warhol, Jackson Pollock and Roy Lichtenstein) and Northwest coast Native American art (composed of nearly 200 masks, sculptures and household items). Temporary exhibitions are similarly diverse. A dynamic events calendar helps distinguish the museum, offering up a bevy of concerts, films, lectures, family programs and classes. Admission is waived on the first Thursday of every month, and a restaurant and two gift shops are onsite.
Tuesday-Wednesday and Sunday 10 a.m.-5 p.m., Thursday-Friday 10 a.m.-9 p.m.

## TIME IT

### Bumbershoot
*Seattle Center, 206-281-7788; www.bumbershoot.com*
This annual multi-day music fest is among the largest of its kind on the West Coast. Legendary artists and rising stars alike perform in more than 30 different indoor and outdoor venues, stages and galleries. Bumbershoot also features poetry, dance, comedy and contemporary art exhibits. Labor Day weekend.

### Fremont Oktoberfest
*Fremont District, 35th Avenue and Phinney Avenue N., Seattle; www.fremontoktoberfest.org*
The eccentric Fremont neighborhood puts its own stamp on the traditional Bavarian beer-drinking festival with a rambunctious chainsaw pumpkin-carving contest, a 5k run and live bands that run the gamut from mainstream to bizarre. This street fair is considered one of the top Oktoberfest festivals outside of Germany, and it takes place over the course of the third weekend in September. The rowdy beer garden is quite a sight, serving a wide variety of beers (including root beer for kids) with an emphasis on local microbrews. Late September.

## Passport to Woodinville
*www.woodinvillewinecountry.com*
The Passport event is like a big open house for local wineries. Flash your pre-paid passport at a participating winery to gain entry and get a libation and some food. Always a sell-out event, overcrowding can be a problem. But by your fourth stop, you won't even notice. April.

## Saint Nicholas Day
*www.woodinvillewinecountry.com*
Nothing makes you feel more jolly than wine. So get full of the holiday spirit at this holiday-themed event, where you can taste samples from exclusive boutique wineries that are normally closed to the public, as well as special selections from a few of Woodinville's more well-known participants. December.

# CHAPTER 6
# CANADA OKANAGAN VALLEY

Quails' Gate Vineyards • CedarCreek Estate Winery • CedarCreek Estate Wines • Spirit Ridge at Nk'Mip Cellars

Oenophiles will have a crush on this region nestled in the heart of British Columbia, four hours from Vancouver. The wineries of Okanagan Valley have well-earned the area's nickname as "The Napa of the North," though many of them lack the attitude of their Northern California peers. The valley, which also has hundreds of orchards, offers some 120 wineries, holds wine festivals year-round and rewards the area's best with a VQA (Vintners Quality Alliance) bottle seal, which requires the approval of an expert tasting panel. B.C.'s largest and oldest wine-growing area—which includes Kelowna, Oliver, Summerland, Osoyoos and Penticton—produces a number of varietals, such as pinot noir, pinot gris, merlot and riesling. Its hot, dry climate and varied geography explain the diverse wine offerings. There are snowy mountains, sandy beaches, lakes and Canada's only desert, the Sonoran. Since it gets more sun than any other part of B.C., the Okanagan Valley is a great place for outdoor activities. Hiking and biking are popular, as are water sports—just watch out for Ogopogo, Lake Okanagan's own Loch Ness monster. Whichever sport you choose, it'll help break up the many winery tours throughout the valley. That's where your own crush on the valley itself will begin.

INNISKILLIN OKANAGAN VINEYARDS

## TASTE

### Burrowing Owl Estate Winery
*100 Burrowing Owl Place, Oliver, 877-498-0620; www.bovwine.ca*
Since Burrowing Owl is in one of Canada's most endangered ecosystems, the locals hold a special concern for the surrounding habitat. The winery's name pays homage to the area's endangered desert and grasslands bird that roosts and nests in already dug burrows. Burrowing Owl uses environmentally safe fertilizers, relocates snakes that happen to slither onto the property instead of killing them and employs nature's own form of pest control in the form of 100 bluebird boxes and two bat nurseries on the vineyards. All of this goes a long way in making the winery's yummy cabernet franc and cabernet sauvignon—which both took silver medals in the 2008 New World International Wine competition—go down even easier. To get the full Burrowing Owl experience, stay in the property's guesthouse, which comes equipped with a pool, a hot tub and airy rooms overlooking the vineyards. For more wine-related fun, order in-room spa treatments such as the Essential Chardonnay manicure or the merlot-scented Wine Country scrub.
Daily 10 a.m.-5 p.m. Closed January 2-February 14.

### CedarCreek Estate Winery
*5445 Lakeshore Road, Kelowna, 250-764-8866; www.cedarcreek.bc.ca*
In 1986, British Columbian Senator Ross Fitzpatrick acquired a small winery and apple orchard along the hills of Kelowna, but he didn't want to mix apples and grapes. Instead, he converted it all into a vineyard. It was a good hunch, since the family-owned CedarCreek went on to win numerous accolades. Almost half of the vineyard's 50 acres are devoted to CedarCreek's signature wine, pinot noir. Pair it with wine-friendly food at the CedarCreek's Vineyard Terrace Restaurant (open June-September). The alfresco eatery wraps around the wine shop, which is helpful in case you find your glass suddenly empty. Watch the sun set against the picturesque mountains as you tipple, and if you are lucky, you might catch a concert on the terrace, which will provide a nice soundtrack for the evening.
Daily November-April 11 a.m.-5 p.m., May-October 10 a.m.-6 p.m.

PATIO VIEW AT QUAIL'S GATE

### Dirty Laundry Vineyard
*7311 Fiske St., Summerland, 250-494-8815; www.dirtylaundry.ca*
This cheeky boutique winery rests high on a plateau overlooking the original Summerland township, just 50 minutes from Kelowna. Though one of the newer kids on the block, it's already produced some award-winners, most notably for its riesling and three gewürztraminer varietals. From the patio—which is shaded by a canopy of vines—you'll be able to see Okanagan Lake, the Trestle Bridge and, if you time it right, the Kettle Valley Steam Train in high season. Check the events portion of the Web site or call prior to going—during the summer, the vineyard hosts live music concerts. Daily 10 a.m.-5 p.m. Call for off-season hours.

### Inniskillin Okanagan Vineyards
*Road 11, Oliver, 250-498-6663; www.inniskillin.com*
Like its sister winery in the Niagara Peninsula, the British Columbia outpost of Inniskillin specializes in ice wine. This dessert wine is made by picking frozen grapes and pressing them before they thaw, a process that yields only a few precious drops of concentrated liquid to use for the wine. Originally a German drink and known as Eiswein, ice wine has become one of Canada's more tasty exports, and Inniskillin's brand is sold in more than 59 countries. The founders of the company are the unlikely godfathers of Canadian wine. Austrian-born chemist Karl Kaiser and Italian-Canadian agriculture graduate Donald Ziraldo started their winery in a converted packing shed. Despite the winery's modest setting, the duo's wine got a lot of attention. The pair no longer runs the company, as Kaiser retired and Ziraldo went on to be the founding chair of the Vintners Quality Alliance. But their legacy lives on at this Okanagan vineyard, which is only about 12 miles north of the Washington State border.
Daily winter 10 a.m.-4 p.m., summer 10 a.m.-5 p.m.

CANADA

### Mission Hill Family Estate
*1730 Mission Hill Road, Westbank, 250-768-6448; www.missionhillwinery.com*
Perched atop a hill, the Mission Hill Family Estate offers stunning views of Lake Okanagan and its own vineyards of chardonnay and pinot noir grapes. The only thing that rivals the scenery is the winery's architecture. When you enter the estate through the imposing arches and keystone, you'll see a contemporary take on an old-time mission. Mission Hill boasts a 12-story bell tower; the Chagall Room, a reception hall that showcases a rare tapestry from the Russian artist; and a cellar that was formed by underground volcanic rock. But you won't want to spend your time indoors. Head to the open-air Terrace restaurant or the outdoor amphitheatre to catch a concert, dance performance, movie or play. Also be sure to grab a glass of Oculus, Mission Hill's signature Bordeaux-inspired wine, for the outing.
Daily 10 a.m.-6 p.m. Call for off-season hours.

*Burrowing Owl Estate Winery • Quail's Gate • Patio at Nk'Mip • Dining at Sumac Ridge Estate Winery*

### Nk'Mip Cellars
*1400 Rancher Creek Road, Osoyoos, 250-495-2985; www.nkmipcellars.com*
Created by Osoyoos Indians, Nk'Mip (pronounced "in-ka-meep") is North America's first aboriginal-owned winery. The lakeside winery, located in Canada's only desert, is just one component of a massive one-stop tourist destination. Stay in a luxurious villa at the Spirit Ridge Vineyard Resort and Spa or rough it at Nk'Mip's Campground and RV Park. Onsite amenities include a nine-hole golf course and a spa featuring an aboriginal-inspired Dreamcatcher aromatherapy massage. You can learn more about the area's native traditions and one of Canada's endangered ecosystems at the Nk'Mip Desert Cultural Centre. Just don't forget to indulge in the best offering of all: Nk'Mip's award-winning chardonnay, pinot blanc, merlot and pinot noir.
Daily winter 10 a.m.-4 p.m., summer 9 a.m.-5 p.m.

### Quails' Gate
*3303 Boucherie Road, Kelowna, 800-420-9463; www.quailsgate.com*
The Stewart family, which settled in the Okanagan Valley in 1908, took its love for red wine to the next level by opening this vineyard in the 1980s. Still family-owned, the winery is known for its award-winning pinot noir, but has expanded into whites, with chardonnay as another one of its trademark vinos. Aside from the wine, visitors come to Quails' Gate to eat at Old Vines

CEDARCREEK VINEYARDS

WINE BARRELS AT INNISKILLIN

Restaurant, which has a seasonal menu tailored for food-and-wine pairings and a patio that offers lovely views of the vineyard. After you've gorged yourself, walk it off around the lush garden. You may catch a whiff of lavender or trumpet vine, but your sniffer likely will be overwhelmed with the more than 500 roses on the grounds. Among the plants and flowers, you'll find the 100-year-old cabin that houses the Wineshop. Stop in for a nightcap.

Daily year-round, hours vary.

### Sumac Ridge Estate Winery
*17403 Highway 97N, Summerland, 250-494-0451; www.sumacridge.com*

Sumac is pushing 30, and in this young but prolific wine-producing region, that makes it one of the oldest wineries. But this is the right industry in which to be of-age, and the winery has several advantages over its younger neighbors: it was one of the region's ice wine pioneers, and it was the first to produce meritage outside of the U.S. Stand-out wines include gewürztraminer and riesling, which come from grapes grown on a gently rolling vineyard near Lake Okanagan, and cabernet sauvignon, pinot blanc and merlot (grown in the 115-acre Black Sage Vineyard just south of Okanagan). The winery's onsite restaurant, Cellar Door Bistro, serves regional cuisine that's also locally sourced, which means that as you sit on the patio with a spectacular view of a shimmering Lake Okanagan, you'll feel like you're not just tasting the valley's bounty, but living it.

Daily April-October 9 a.m.-9 p.m., January-February 9 a.m.-5 p.m., November-December and March, Tuesday-Saturday 9 a.m.-8:30 p.m., Sunday-Monday 9 a.m.-5 p.m.

### Summerhill Pyramid Winery
*4870 Chute Lake Road, Kelowna, 250-764-8000, 800-667-3538; www.summerhill.bc.ca*

Who says wine and new age don't mix? Okay, maybe nobody says that, and that's probably why Summerhill is so successful as Canada's largest certified organic vineyard. Founder and owner Stephen Cipes quit his job in 1987 and moved to the Valley from New York to test whether metaphysical energy would affect an old-world practice. To this day, Summerhill ages wine inside a giant

pyramid on the shores of Okanagan Lake. The winery consistently wins awards for its ice wine and bruts, though it'd be downright silly not to try one of the organically grown varietals, which include rieslings, chardonnays, pinot noirs and gewürtztraminers. The onsite bistro cooks up delicious dishes using organic veggies grown on the property.
Daily April-December 9 a.m.-9 p.m., January-March 9 a.m.-5 p.m.

# TOURS

All wineries offer property tours. Check with the individual wineries for more information.

### Monashee Adventure Tours
*1591 Highland Drive North, Kelowna, 250-762-9253, 888-762-9253; www.monasheeadventuretours.com*

If you prefer traveling via two-wheeler, Monashee leads 10 different winery bike tours to accommodate all levels of riders. The daylong South Okanagan Wine Country Cycle Tour hits Kelowna and Oliver—two Okanagan Valley biggies—and the Sonoran Desert, as well as two wineries. To change things up a bit, try the Peddle and Paddle Tour, where you ride to Okanagan Lake, canoe to shore and then head to a winery for lunch and a tour.

### Okanagan Wine Country Tours
*1310 Water St., Kelowna, 250-868-9463, 866-689-9463; www.okwinetours.com*

Duffers should sign up for the Chip & Sip, a tour that splits the day between wineries and pre-selected golf courses, with transportation provided to both. The more adventurous will take the Floatplane Wine Tours, which include a 45-minute ride that ends with a landing on Osoyoos Lake. From there, a guide will escort you to a custom-designed luxury vehicle as you shuttle off to five award-winning wineries and end with lunch at Burrowing Owl Estate Winery.

### TRK Helicopter Charters
*5225 216th St., Unit 102, Hangar 12, Langley, 604-533-4150, 888-875-4354; www.trkheli.com*

There are only so many walking tours you can do before your poor legs give out. Give them a rest by touring the Okanagan Valley via helicopter. TRK's Helicopter Winery Tour will show you an incredible aerial view of the region's snow-capped mountains as you fly to the highly rated Mission Hill Family Estate. There, a sommelier will guide you through the vineyards with breaks for nibbles and wine. Then you'll fuel up with a three-course lunch at Mission Hill's alfresco Terrace restaurant before getting back on the chopper. Last stop: Golden Ears National Park to see 8,000-foot peaks and 500-foot waterfalls. You'll get a final photo op when you stop off near one of these sites—and some bubbly, too.

FOUR SEASONS HOTEL VANCOUVER

## STAY

A visit to the Okanagan Valley could begin or end with a stay in Vancouver about four hours to the west.

### ★★★Coast Capri Hotel

*1171 Harvey Ave., Kelowna, 250-860-6060, 800-716-6199; www.coasthotels.com*
Surrounded by mountains and orchards, this Kelowna landmark is near golf courses, water sports and Lake Okanagan. After working up an appetite in the heated outdoor pool or hot tub, grab dinner at the hotel's Vintage Room, which offers dishes that complement local VQA wines. End the evening with a visit to Bluelines Sport & Comedy Club, where the Canadian stand-up comedy chain Yuk Yuk's takes over Thursdays to Saturdays.
185 rooms. High-speed Internet access. Two restaurants, bar, coffee bar. Fitness center. Spa. Pool. Business center. Pets accepted. $

### ★★★★Four Seasons Hotel Vancouver

*791 W. Georgia St., Vancouver, 604-689-9333; www.fourseasons.com/vancouver*
Located in the hub of the city, the Four Seasons Hotel Vancouver is connected via the lobby to the underground Pacific Centre mall, so you won't even need an umbrella to go shopping during the rainy Pacific Northwest winter. A mere block from Robson Street, a favorite shopping spot for Vancouverites and visitors alike, the Four Seasons is a five-minute walk to the Vancouver Art Gallery and a 10-minute stroll to Coal Harbour's restaurants. But if you want to kick back with some wine, look no further than the hotel's sleek YEW restaurant + bar, which offers more than 150 by the glass. When making a reservation, request a room on an upper floor facing north and you'll awake to a sublime alpine panorama (on a clear day). Take advantage of the rooms' iPod docking stations to start the day with your favorite tunes instead of a jarring wake-up call.
372 rooms. Wireless Internet access. Restaurants/bar. Fitness center. Spa. Pool. Business center. Pets accepted. $$$

CANADA

## ★★★★The Sutton Place Hotel
*845 Burrard St., Vancouver, 604-682-5511, 866-378-8866; www.suttonplace.com*
Smack-dab in the business and shopping core of downtown Vancouver, this hotel offers guest rooms that exude a European flavor, while the dining and lounge areas feature comfortable Old World motifs. If the samples at the wineries don't loosen you up, treat yourself to the Thai massage at the luxurious Vida Wellness Spa—it'll relax you in no time. And if you're still thirsty for vino, head to the Sutton Place Wine Merchant. Among its stock of 500 labels are exclusive brands and British Columbian specialties.
397 rooms. Wireless Internet access. Restaurant, bar. Fitness center. Spa. Pool. Business center. Pets accepted. $$$

### The Cove Lakeside Resort
*4205 Gellatly Road, Westbank, 877-762-2683; www.covelakeside.com*
Situated between popular Kelowna and tiny Peachland, and just 10 minutes from the must-see Mission Hill Family Estate, the Cove Lakeside Resort seems to have it all. And it does: a hotel with lakeside pools, a slide and hot tubs, all for kiddies and adults; a tennis court; beachside fire pits; a movie theater; an activity center for teens; a Bikram yoga studio; a putting green; and a private marina. If you can't decide what to do, just go back to your room, snuggle by the fireplace and watch a movie on the plasma TV. But first, uncork a couple of bottles that you brought back from Mission Hill and stored in your kitchen's wine fridge.
150 rooms. Wireless Internet access. Restaurant, bar. Fitness center. Spa. Pool. $$

### Summerland Waterfront Resort
*13011 Lakeshore Drive S., Summerland, 250-494-8180, 877-494-8111; www.summerlandresorthotel.com*
The new Summerland Waterfront Resort's modern guest rooms have full kitchens, dining and living room areas, fireplaces, balconies and great linens. But the hotel's best asset may be its location. Summerland is a quaint town in the Okanagan Valley that's a good midway point between Kelowna and Osoyoos. Plus, the Summerland Waterfront Resort is just steps away from the water. Take to the lake and rent a boat or Jet Ski. If you're more of a foodie than a water warrior, the resort offers Culinary Adventures Packages, where you attend hands-on wine-friendly cooking classes in the Hainle Vineyard's master kitchen. And if you want to get cooking in your hotel room's kitchen, Hainle's chefs will come to you for a private lesson.
115 rooms. Wireless Internet access. Restaurant. Fitness center. Spa. Pool. Business center. $$

## EAT

### ★★★★Bishop's
*2183 W. Fourth Ave., Vancouver, 604-738-2025; www.bishopsonline.com*
Bishop's houses the most coveted tables in Vancouver. Intimate, modern and airy, this chic restaurant is known for a West Coast continental menu that emphasizes seasonal, organic produce and British Columbian seafood, and has spawned several cookbooks, including *Fresh*, which focuses on local, sustainable foods. Choose among the extensive wine list to find a bottle to help wash down a plate of seared B.C. halibut or wild Pacific salmon.
International menu. Reservations recommended. Outdoor seating. $$$

POOL DECK AT COAST CAPRI HOTEL

### ★★★★La Belle Auberge
*4856 48th Ave., Ladner, 604-946-7717; www.labelleauberge.com*
If you crave the glorious food of France's best kitchens, make the 30-minute drive from Vancouver to the town of Ladner and dine at La Belle Auberge. Set in a charming 1905 country house, the intimate restaurant is composed of five antique-filled salon-style dining rooms. The kitchen, led by executive chef/owner and masterful culinary technician Bruno Marti, offers authentic French cuisine.
French menu. Reservations recommended. Outdoor seating. $$$

### ★★★★Lumière
*2551 W. Broadway, Vancouver, 604-739-8185; www.lumiere.ca*
Lumière is a glossy, elegant restaurant that offers European-style dining under the guidance of new chef Dale MacKay, whose last stint was at Gordon Ramsay at The London-New York. The menu offers French cuisine with Asian accents as well as a healthy respect for regional ingredients. The global wine list is impressive and the bartenders' concoctions recalls a pre-Prohibition era when the craft of the cocktail was taken as seriously as the mastery of the plate. The popular new tasting bar offers drinks and small plates.
French menu. Reservations recommended. Outdoor seating. $$$$

### ★★★★West
*2881 Granville St., Vancouver, 604-738-8938; www.westrestaurant.com*
West is one of those sleek, heavenly spots that makes sipping wine for hours on end an easy task. The temperature-controlled wall of wine is a highlight of the restaurant, which makes room for Old World producers, rare bottles and New World vintners. The restaurant is an ideal choice for gourmands in search of an inventive, eclectic meal, as well as those who crave regional flavor and seasonal ingredients.
Continental menu. Reservations recommended. $$$

# CANADA

## Bliss Bakery

*4200 Beach Ave., Peachland, 250-767-2711; www.blissbakery.ca*
While traveling, stop in the blink-and-you'll-miss-it town of Peachland to pick up fresh gourmet sandwiches, cookies and other all-natural treats from Bliss Bakery. The artisan bakery doesn't use any chemicals, preservatives or hydrogenated oils in its handmade-from-scratch goodies. If you have time, bring the food across the street for a lakeside picnic.
Bakery menu. $

## Bouchons

*1180 Sunset Drive, Kelowna, 250-763-6595; www.bouchonsbistro.com*
While perusing the menu of traditional French specialties at Bouchons, you'll notice a stone hut in the middle of the maroon-and-gold room. The structure is actually a climate-controlled "cellar" that houses more than 170 different labels from local vineyards and beyond. If you need help finding a wine to pair with your cassoulet, the restaurant's two onsite sommeliers will help.
French menu. Reservations recommended. Outdoor seating. $$

*Four Seasons Hotel Vancouver ▪ Lumière ▪ West ▪ Dining at Lumière*

## The Vanilla Pod Restaurant

*9917A Main St., Summerland, 250-494-8222; www.thevanillapod.ca*
Tucked in the quiet downtown of Summerland, this intimate, earth-toned bistro and wine bar is anything but vanilla. The Vanilla Pod is stocked with local Okanagan Valley VQA vintages that pair well with executive chef Bruno Terroso's excellent tapas. The regional cuisine uses locally grown and organic ingredients with a sprinkle of ethnic touches.
International menu. Reservations recommended. $$

# SPA

## Absolute Spa at the Century

*1015 Burrard St., Vancouver, 604-684-2772;*
*www.absolutespa.com*
Celebs such as Gwyneth Paltrow and Uma Thurman are fans of this Canadian luxury spa chain. The Century Plaza Hotel's spa has an extensive list of services, including facials, wraps, spa therapy baths, body scrubs and specialty massages, as well as special menus for moms-to-be, teens and men. Get the pink grapefruit-scented Jet Lag Recovery massage, even

ABSOLUTE SPA AT THE CENTURY

PERFECT HEALTH SPA

if you don't have jet lag—this massage will give you a great detox after all those wine tastings. The holly and macadamia seed oils will moisturize your parched skin and the cucumber extract will make you feel refreshed. Don't leave before using the gratis eucalyptus steam rooms and indoor chemical-free swimming pool.

### Perfect Health Spa
*2525 Arbutus St., Vancouver, 604-736-2111; www.perfecthealthspa.ca*
This relaxation haven got the nickname "The Movie Spa" for allowing guests to veg and watch a film while getting manis and pedis. But the movies don't play on some rinky-dink TV hanging from the ceiling. The Vancouver outpost has two rooms with movie screens, the larger of which covers the entire wall. Choose from the spa's DVD collection (or bring your own title), settle into a comfy chair, order up the chocolate manicure and pedicure, and enjoy the show.

## SHOP

### British Columbia Wine Information Centre
*553 Railway St., Penticton, 250-490-2006; www.bcwineinfo.net*
You can learn about the history of Canadian wines at the British Columbia Wine Information Centre, but the real reason to go is the wine shop. In case you don't make it to all of the wineries on your list, you can find most local wines among the shop's well-stocked racks. While you're there, you can also imbibe during free wine tastings and buy some local cheese to pair with your libations. Daily summer 9 a.m.-7 p.m., winter Monday-Saturday 9 a.m.-6 p.m., Sunday 10 a.m.-5 p.m.

### Heritage District, Vancouver
Find your way to Howe and Hastings Streets, and you will be surrounded by luxury chains such as Cartier, Dunhill, Hugo Boss and the local store **Leone** (*757 W. Hastings St., 604-683-1133; www.leone.ca*), which carries the likes of Versace and Escada. A little further east, at Granville and Dunsmuir, just around the corner from the Four Seasons Vancouver, check out the newly redesigned flagship **Holt Renfrew** (*Pacific Centre, 737 Dunsmuir St., 604-681-3121; www.holtrenfrew.*

com). This is the Canadian version of Bloomingdale's and Neiman Marcus, combined—a definite stop for any diehard shopper. Right up the street at the historic Fairmont Hotel, you'll find the luxe retailers Louis Vuitton, Hermès, Tiffany and Coach.

**Robson Street**
*Between Burrard and Jervis Streets, Vancouver; www.robsonstreet.ca*
Vancouver's most famous shopping street, Robson features block after block of neighborhood stores with restaurants and cafés peppered throughout. Stores run the gamut from Ferragamo to Roots and Zara. Weekends and evenings bring street performers and live outdoor entertainment to this shopping strip.

**South Granville**
*2300 Granville St., Vancouver; www.southgranville.org*
If it's boutique shopping you're after, head to the South Granville neighborhood. Tucked among galleries and teashops, upscale stores like Max Mara, DKNY and Williams-Sonoma mix with unique local shops such as **Country Furniture** (*3097 Granville St., Vancouver, 604-738-6411; www.countryfurniture.net*), **Farmhouse Collections** (*2915 Granville St., Vancouver, 604-738-0167; www.farmhousecollections.com*) and **Lothantique** (*2655 Granville St., Vancouver, 604-738-4888; www.lothantique.ca*). First established with the carriage trade in the 1920s, South Granville is now home to more than 200 stores, restaurants and galleries. Stop for a little chocolate pick-me-up at either Daniel le Chocolat Belge or Purdy's, both on Granville Street. Within this neighborhood you'll also find Gallery Row, which is home to more than 30 galleries and antiques stores. Check out the **Douglas Reynolds Gallery** (*2335 Granville St., Vancouver, 604-731-9292; www.douglasreynoldsgallery.com*) for its amazing selection of museum-quality Northwest coast native art and jewelry.

## SEE AND DO

**Arts Club Theatre Company**
*1585 Johnston St., Vancouver, 604-687-1644; www.artsclub.com*
Having helped launch the careers of actors Michael J. Fox and Brent Carver, the Arts Club Theatre steals the Vancouver stage spotlight. In addition to its year-round mainstage productions—classics, comedies and musicals—at Stanley Industrial Alliance Stage (Granville and W. 12th), the company mounts productions at the Granville Island Stage.

**Ballet British Columbia**
*677 Davie St., Vancouver, 604-732-5003; www.balletbc.com*
With a company 17 dancers strong, Ballet B.C. reigns as Vancouver's top dance troupe. Directed by John Alleyne, a former dancer with the Stuttgart Ballet and the National Ballet of Canada, the company's repertoire includes works by such famed choreographers as William Forsythe and John Cranko, as well as commissioned works by Canadian talents. Ballet B.C.'s home stage is the Queen Elizabeth Theatre (Hamilton and Dunsmuir Streets).

**Kelowna Art Gallery**
*1315 Water St., Kelowna, 250-762-2226; www.kelownaartgallery.com*
Kelowna's downtown Cultural District makes it the arts epicenter of the Okanagan Valley. In the middle of the district is the Kelowna Art Gallery, which showcases works from local, national and international artists in its four exhibition spaces.

KELOWNA ART GALLERY

The permanent collection features contemporary Canadian artists, with a focus on those from Okanagan. If you get inspired looking at the art, drop in to one of the classrooms to create your own masterpiece.
Daily Tuesday-Saturday 10 a.m.-5 p.m., Sunday 1-4 p.m., Thursday evenings until 9 p.m.

### Lake City Casinos
*The Grand Okanagan Resort, 1300 Water St., Kelowna, 250-860-9467; Penticton Lakeside Resort, 21 Lakeshore Drive W., Penticton, 250-487-1280; www.lakecitycasinos.com*
If you're feeling both lucky and kitschy, head to the flagship Kelowna casino. Enter the 20,000-square-foot casino through a waterfall to hop aboard a Caribbean cruise ship-themed gameland. There are the requisite blackjack, roulette and slots, plus Caribbean stud poker (as per the theme, of course). The lakeside Penticton location offers a slight variation on the theme: Caribbean wharfside.

### Vancouver Symphony Orchestra
*601 Smithe St., Vancouver, 604-684-9100; www.vancouversymphony.ca*
As Canada's third-largest orchestra, the Vancouver Symphony presents more than 150 concerts annually, most of them at the ornate Orpheum Theatre. The symphony's programs encompass classical, light classical, pops and children's works. Most concerts are on weekends and include family-oriented matinees. September-June.

## TIME IT

### Festival of the Grape
*Oliver; www.festivalofthegrape.com*
More than 30 wineries are featured in this annual small-town festival, which takes place in Oliver, the self-proclaimed "Wine Capital of Canada" and home to the Golden Mile, a strip that's said to be the best place in which to grow grapes in Okanagan Valley. The fest includes a blessing of the harvest and a grape stomp competition. You should plant yourself in the wine tents

to sample the local libations. Just try not to drink yourself silly, as this is a family-friendly event. October.

### Okanagan Wine Festivals
*Kelowna, 250-861-6654; www.owfs.com*
The Okanagan Wine Festivals Society keeps oenophiles coming back to the valley with a big festival each season. The spring fest happens during the first 10 days in May; the summer festivities take place the second weekend in August; the fall fest is a 10-day event in early October; and the winter Ice Wine Festival occurs in January. Events are usually spread out through the Okanagan Valley and include tastings, classes and gourmet meals.

# UNEXPECTED
# WINE REGIONS

# CHAPTER 7
# LONG ISLAND WINE COUNTRY

*Long Island Sound ▪ Pool at The Baker House 1650 ▪ Channing Daughters Winery ▪ Long Island Beach*

When people think of Long Island, they often conjure up images of strip malls, jam-packed expressways and thick New York accents. True, there is all that, but an afternoon spent in Long Island's East End, one of the fastest growing wine regions in the country, will have you wondering where all of that is. Much like San Francisco's proximity to Napa Valley, Long Island Wine Country is less than two hours from New York City, yet feels eons away. Farm stands line the quiet, country roads, rolling vineyards stretch in every direction, pristine beaches abound and the air offers that fresh, not-so-New-York smell. Whether you're looking for a quick daytrip to get a reprieve from Midtown mayhem or craving a weekend of cozy bed and breakfast living, with exceptional food and wine tossed in, a trip to Long Island should be on every oenophiles' short list.

Getting out to eastern Long Island is akin to a lesson in modern transportation. Planes, trains and automobiles—as well as ferries, buses, boats and helicopters—are all possibilities (some more expensive than others), but the best options are the Long Island Rail Road (*www.lirr.org*), which runs several trains back and forth from New York City daily, or the Hampton Jitney bus service (*www.hamptonjitney.com*). These public transport options allow for a relaxing journey to and from the city, and keep you safely off the road if you've imbibed a tad too vigorously at that last vineyard. If you do

LONG ISLAND VINEYARDS

plan to drive, be warned that weekend traffic in the Hamptons can be fierce.

The east end of Long Island forks at Riverhead, leaving the chic summer playground that is the Hamptons to the south (along with Montauk if you travel far enough out) and a more bucolic, laid-back atmosphere to the north. Bordered by the Atlantic Ocean and the Long Island Sound and separated by the Great Peconic Bay, cool temperatures are guaranteed year-round, enabling a long growing season and ideal soil conditions for merlots, cabernet francs, chardonnays and sauvignon francs. So, ready your palate and head east.

## NORTH FORK

The North Fork contains more than 95 percent of Long Island's wineries, so it's an obvious place to start. Riverhead is the center of the split, and more commercial than some of the towns further east, though no less capable of harvesting full-bodied goodness in a glass. From there, the small towns only get smaller—and quainter—from Aquebogue and Mattituck to Cutchogue and Southold, and if you stick to Routes 48 (north) and 25 (south), you're sure to hit more wineries than you could ever tackle in a weekend. Here are a few good choices along the way.

## TASTE

### Castello di Borghese
*Route 48 and Alvah's Lane, Cutchogue, 631-734-5111;*
*www.castellodiborghese.com*
As Long Island's oldest and most respected winery, Castello di Borghese already had a first-rate reputation when Marco and Ann Marie Borghese purchased it in 1999. They have only added to that lauded repute—enlarging the vineyards, updating the tasting room and creating a cozy seating area for visitors to relax and enjoy their expanded selection of wines. Ann Marie also leads most of the popular winemaker walks herself, strolling

guests through the 84-acre vineyard and into the cellar for an up-close lesson in wine making. As the vineyard boasts the most mature vines in the region, you're best sipping away on their pinot noirs and sauvignon blancs, but the award-winning meritage is a pleasure as well.
Tours: December-June, Saturday 1 p.m., July-November, Thursday and Sunday 1 p.m. Tastings: May-December, Monday-Friday 11 a.m.-5:30 p.m., Saturday 11 a.m.-6 p.m., Sunday 11:30 a.m.-6 p.m., January-April, Thursday-Monday 11 a.m.-5 p.m., closed Tuesday-Wednesday.

### Lieb Family Cellars
*35 Cox Neck Road, Mattituck, 631-298-1942; www.liebcellars.com*
Along Route 48, the Lieb Family Cellars is a popular stop for those who love white wine. Earth-friendly farming has been a crucial part of this vineyard since its inception in 1992, using self-sustainable techniques including hand-tending and herbicide-free grapes. The winery produces chardonnays, merlots and cabernet francs, but the prize goes to their pinot blanc reserves, a refreshing wine with citrus hints and a clean finish. The modern

*Long Island Wine Country • Steak at The Seafood Barge • Castello di Borghese • Channing Daughters Winery*

tasting room offers a casual atmosphere and a constantly changing tasting menu of old and new vintages, so you never know what you'll be treated to. Daily 11 a.m.-5:30 p.m., reservations recommended.

### Martha Clara Vineyards
*6025 Sound Ave., Riverhead, 631-298-0075; www.marthaclaravineyards.com*
Martha Clara Vineyards is no stranger to success. Owned by Robert Entenmann, of Entenmann baking fame, the winery has grown from an 18-acre hobby to more than 100 acres of award-winning vines. Aim to visit on a weekend to enjoy a horse-drawn carriage tour around the property, including where the grapes are grown. The sizeable tasting room can be intimidating, but ask for their Reserve Merlot and you can't go wrong. Sunday-Friday 11 a.m.-5:30 p.m., Saturday 11 a.m.-7 p.m. Call for off-season hours.

WÖLFFER ESTATE MERLOT

WÖLFFER ESTATE TASTING ROOM

### Osprey's Dominion Vineyards
*44075 Main Road, Peconic, 631-765-6188; www.ospreysdominion.com*

If the thought of strawberry wine entices you—hey, no one's judging—a drive out to Osprey's Dominion is well worth the trip. Named after the soaring birds that fly overhead, Osprey's Dominion resides on 90 acres of fruitful soil. Pack a picnic and head to the patio out back (after you've treated yourself to a tasting, of course) to enjoy complimentary live music on the weekends and a seemingly endless horizon over the fields. While you can't go wrong with any of their cabernets or chardonnays, an evening feast is not complete until one of Osprey's delectable dessert wines has been poured.
Daily 11 a.m.-6 p.m., Friday-Saturday until 9 p.m. Call for off-season hours.

### Pindar Vineyards
*37645 Main Road, Peconic, 631-734-6200; www.pindar.net*

Further east on Route 25, Pindar is Long Island's largest vineyard with nearly 550 acres of rich, loamy property, a stunning feat since the estate was founded on only 30 acres of uncultivated land in 1979. With 16 different varietals and more than 60,000 cases produced each year, Pindar draws scores of visitors thanks to the sheer number of choices. Other fans come for the pavilion, an outdoor space often aflutter with live concerts, festivals and epicurean events. If all this wine tasting puts you in a shopping mood, the well-stocked gift boutique is the place to find wine accessories you barely knew existed.

Daily 11 a.m.-5:30 p.m. Check the Web site for Pindar pavilion activities.

## STAY

### The Coffey House Bed and Breakfast
*5705 Main Road, East Marion, 631-477-2107; www.thecoffeyhouse.com*

If you're in search of a picturesque romantic getaway, look no further than The Coffey House in East Marion. The restored 1886 farmhouse serves a daily three-course breakfast and is only 15 minutes away from more than 25 award-winning wineries. Enjoy the hospitality of hosts Rick and Ellie Coffey as you relax in one of the four elegant rooms, each with its own private bath. Outdoor activities include hiking, walking trails, kayaking and swimming. At the end of the day, cozy up in the sitting room in an oversized chair by the fireplace.

4 rooms. High-speed wireless Internet access. Children over 12 years only. Complimentary breakfast. $$$

### Harborfront Inn at Greenport

*209 Front St., Greenport,
631-477-0707;
www.theharborfrontinn.com*

After a day of eastward vineyard hopping, continue on to Greenpoint, and the Harborfront Inn. Smack dab in the middle of an 18th century seaport town, this modern, luxe hotel melds the nostalgic with the contemporary, resulting in one of the premier properties on the North Fork. The spacious guest rooms have custom cherry wood furnishings and include Frette linens, flat-screen TVs and deluxe showers with massaging body sprays. Splurge for the Terrace suite and enjoy a private 900-square-foot terrace with views of Greenport Harbor and Shelter Island. The complimentary continental breakfast is best enjoyed in the lobby with the morning paper, a cup of joe and the crackling of the smoldering fireplace in the background.

35 rooms. Wireless Internet access. Complimentary continental breakfast. Restaurant, bar. Fitness center. Pool. $$$$

### Seatuck Cove House

*61 South Bay Ave., Eastport,
631-325-3300;
www.seatuckcovehouse.com*

Known as Long Island's most elegant waterfront bed and breakfast, Seatuck Cove House overlooks the beautiful Moriches Bay and Seatuck Cove from its 900 feet of waterfront property. All five of the sizeable rooms offer panoramic water views. The Suite Road room is filled with luxurious amenities, complete with a temperature-controlled whirlpool tub, a flat-screen TV, high ceilings and a stone fireplace. Take a dip in the heated pool or frolic along the small, private beach.

5 rooms. Wireless Internet access. Long Island Rail Road transportation available. Pool. $$$$

### The Surf Lodge

*183 Edgemere St., Montauk,
631-668-2632; www.thesurflodge.com*

The words celebrity and hip do not generally describe Montauk. Thanks to The Surf Lodge, that may soon change. Whitewashed walls, sun-bleached pine flooring and subtle surf accents make this hotel the new place to escape for Manhattanites fleeing the city heat. Complete with a restaurant, bar, boutique and hair salon, The Surf Lodge is a one-stop vacation. Relax on The Deck, a 2,600-square-foot outdoor lounge area where you can sip cocktails, hear live music performances on weekends and practice yoga on Sunday mornings from 8 to 9:30 a.m. Indulge in a little celebrity spotting at The Restaurant, as *Top Chef*'s resident cutie-pie Sam Talbot prepares your meal.

32 rooms. Wireless Internet access. Restaurant, bar. $$$$

## EAT

### The Frisky Oyster

*27 Front St., Greenport, 631-477-4265;
www.thefriskyoyster.com*

Aside from an appetizer called oysters Friskafella, you won't find much in the way of oysters here, but this restaurant's original dishes are sure to satisfy your palate.

THE COFFEY HOUSE

Surrounded by votive candles on the table, fabric-covered walls and rich wooden floors, the place has the ambiance of a Manhattan restaurant. The menu changes daily and includes touches of Asian, French and Mexican culinary techniques. Try the wild mushroom and goat cheese quesadilla or the proscuitto-wrapped sea scallops with sautéed spinach and white bean ragout. Finish off the night with the delectable chocolate soufflé cake with mint crème anglaise.
Seafood menu. Dinner. Business casual attire. Reservations recommended. $$$

### The Seafood Barge
*62980 Main Road (Route 25), Southold, 631-765-3010; www.seafoodbarge.com*
Don't let the unassuming exterior of The Seafood Barge fool you. Situated in the Port of Egypt Marina, the restaurant has beautiful waterfront views that provide the perfect backdrop for a casual dining experience. Enjoy traditional seafood favorites like New England clam chowder alongside imaginative dishes such as the pan-seared ahi tuna with fresh peas, asparagus, cipollini onions in a soy reduction. And with reasonable prices, you'll be able to snag an extra bottle of cabernet at your next stop.
Seafood menu. Lunch, dinner. Casual attire. $$

## SHOP

### Verbena
*123 Main St., Greenport, 631-477-4080; www.verbena.net*
Self-described as carrying everything from the sublime to the ridiculous, this one-stop gift shop has everything from Moleskine notebooks to Pré de Provence bath products to Alexis Bittar jewelry. You may find yourself wondering how you previously lived without a mobile clip photo hanger or bendable book light, but one thing is for certain: You won't escape empty-handed.
Call for hours.

# LONG ISLAND

### The Village Cheese Shop
*105 Love Lane, Mattituck,
631-298-8556;
www.thevillagecheeseshop.com*
Cheese lovers will think they have discovered utopia upon stepping into this local storefront. The long counter that greets you boasts fromage from all over the world, as well as a selection of domestic varieties. You can pick up a few wedges to go or stay for a cheese plate or fondue in the onsite café.
Call for hours.

## SOUTH FORK
After a jaunt on the North Fork, why not skip down to the South by taking the ferry from Greenport to Sag Harbor via Shelter Island? It may take some time during the summer, when there are long lines for the ferry, but it will allow you to see a different side of the East End and award you with some great photo ops from the boat.

The South Fork, often overshadowed by the glitz of the Hamptons, has become synonymous with A-list celebrities, convertible traffic jams and jaw-dropping surfside mansions. And, for nearly eight weeks every summer, that repute is surprisingly accurate. There is another side to the South Fork, however—even during the summer months. Wineries, cozy bed and breakfasts and spotless, sandy beaches are cropping up and people are beginning to
take notice.

Once you arrive in Sag Harbor, put your wine cap back on because one of the best wineries on Long Island (and one of only a handful on the South Fork) is right down the road.

# TASTE

### Channing Daughters Winery
*1927 Scuttlehole Road, Bridgehampton, 631-537-7224
www.channingdaughters.com*
This 28-acre winery produces a host of wines, such as pinot grigio, tocai friulano, merlot and chardonnay. Although small, South Fork's Channing Daughters has some special touches, like a discounted wine club and a wood sculpture garden that showcases the art of owner Walter Channing. The winery offers wine tasting classes from May to October. Daily 11 a.m.-5 p.m., closed Tuesdays-Wednesdays, October-April.

### Wölffer Estate Vineyard
*139 Sagg Road, Sagaponack,
631-537-5106; www.wolffer.com*
This Tuscan-style winery is more reminiscent of an enchanted European estate than a vineyard in the Hamptons, but the harvests are decidedly American. The local soil acts as the perfect host for Wölffer's slow-growing vines, and the cool climate, thanks in part to the close proximity to the Atlantic, allows for late harvests and strong, natural acidity. A visit to the estate is a special affair: immaculately manicured grounds and a trickling, circular fountain greet you as you make your way into the impressive 12,000-square-foot winery. While the winemaking facilities make their home on the lower level, the main floor impresses with terracotta tiling, antique stained-glass windows and massive French doors that open onto the vineyards. Sit, imbibe on a glass of crisp chardonnay and take in the spectacular view, all as you remind yourself that you're farther from Italy than you might seem. See Web site for hours and special events.

THE BAKER HOUSE 1650

## STAY

### The Baker House 1650
*181 Main St., East Hampton, 631-324-4081; www.bakerhouse1650.com*
With the elegance of a country estate and the amenities of a luxury hotel, this is a great pick for those who appreciate the finer details, including Bose radios and CD players, L'Occitane toiletries and claw foot tubs in some rooms. Designed in 1910 and modeled after a 1648 farmhouse, the manor has been decorated with period antiques and wood-paneled rooms, and the surrounding landscape is awash in verdant gardens. After a day at the beach or strolling through town, relax in the spa before enjoying an evening cocktail by the pool.
7 rooms. Wireless Internet access. Complimentary breakfast. Spa. Pool. $$$$

## EAT

### Bridgehampton Candy Kitchen
*Main and School Streets, Bridgehampton, 631-537-9885*
This classic luncheonette is always packed with locals, and for good reason—the food is good and the prices are even better. Open since the 1920s, the Candy Kitchen serves simple, tasty fare like burgers and fries, and made-to-order skillet omelets. Be a kid again and order a malt or fountain soda that's tasty enough to make you giddy.
American menu. Breakfast, lunch, dinner. Casual attire. No credit cards accepted. $

### Della Femina
*99 North Main St., East Hampton, 631-329-6666; www.dellafemina.com*
The celebrity caricatures that greet you upon entering this New American eatery hint at the see-and-be-seen reputation that it carries during summer months. In the off-season, it maintains a more mellow existence, serving consistently good food and reasonably priced prix fixe menus to locals and the occasional tourist. Regulars often stick to oysters on the half shell and the Maine day boat halibut with local asparagus and a parsnip purée, but

carnivores will enjoy the rack of lamb with Dijon and brioche bread crust, goat cheese and celery root gratin. For dessert, you can't go amiss with the house made gelato and sorbet.

New American menu. Dinner. Winter Brunch. Bar. Business casual attire. Reservations required in summer. $$$

## SHOP

### Collette Consignment
*89 Jobs Lane, Southampton, 631-204-9511; www.colletteconsignment.com*
Don't let the word consignment fool you. This Hamptons relic isn't for the penny-pincher; labels run from Chanel to Ungaro, Dolce & Gabbana to Jimmy Choo, and it's all vintage fabulous. The development of a celeb following has only added to the couture collection, with stars dumping their to-die-for wardrobes for new and improved wares. You may be asking for trouble upon entering this designer mecca, but you'll certainly be well-dressed trouble by the time you leave.
Call for hours.

*The Seafood Barge ▪ Hamptons Beach ▪ Long Island Boats ▪ Wölffer Estate*

# CHAPTER 8
# TEXAS HILL COUNTRY

*Fonda San Miguel ▪ Trio Restaurant ▪ LakeHouse Spa at Lake Austin Spa Resort ▪ GrapeCreek Winery*

Texas is famous for its barbecue 'n' beer culinary heritage, which is why its burgeoning winery scene is delightfully surprising—in fact, the Texas Hill Country American Viticultural Area is the second largest AVA in the U.S., covering more than 15,000 miles. Driving west from the state capital of Austin, you'll notice a change in landscape: rolling hills, wildflowers, limestone formations and quaint little towns of European descent. Adding to Hill Country's bohemian vibe is its long-standing reputation as a haven for country music fans, artists and weekend ranchers and homeowners. Still, it was not until the '70s that the first modern-day vineyard sprung up at Fall Creek.

An amazing winery renaissance has taken place since then. Two of the most exciting towns in this region are Marble Falls—with its beautiful lakes, rolling hills and nearby wineries—and Fredericksburg, originally a German community and now a bustling town with shops, restaurants and tasting rooms. The area in the heart of Texas now boasts more than 20 wineries and numerous vineyards. And, nothing washes down killer Texas barbecue like a bottle of vino from the Lonestar State.

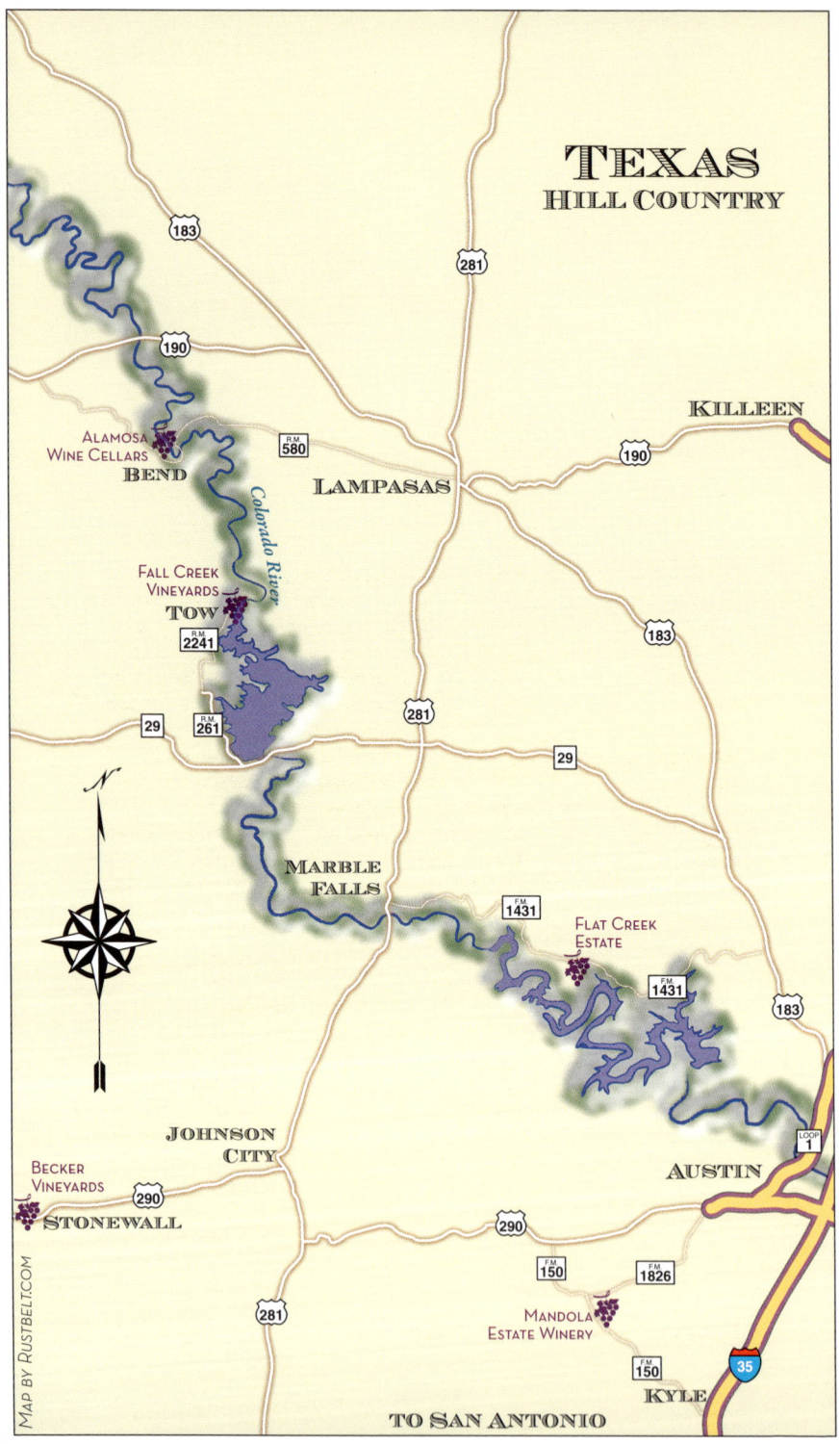

FREDERICKSBURG FIELDS

## TASTE

### Alamosa Wine Cellars
*677 County Road 430, Bend, 325-628-3313; www.alamosawinecellars.com*
Alamosa Wine Cellars is located near the tiny town of Bend, about an hour and a half north of Marble Falls. Jim (who graduated from the University of California, Davis with a degree in fermentation science….yes, that's an actual degree) and Karen Davis began Alamosa with a simple premise that the best wines in Texas could be made from grapes best suited for the region's climate and soil (as opposed to those who just rush to plant their favorites, like cabernet sauvignon and chardonnay, which have had mixed results in the state). Makes sense. And there certainly won't be any complaining when you're sitting on the large veranda overlooking the 10-acre vineyard, sipping on El Guapo (a tempranillo-based blend with an intriguing bouquet of blueberry pie and new saddle leather), Texacaia (a Super Texan with sangiovese, syrah and tempranillo) and Scissortail (a white, rhone-style blend of marsanne, roussanne and viognier).
Friday-Saturday 10 a.m.-5 p.m.; Sundays noon-5 p.m.

### Becker Vineyards
*464 Becker Farms Road, Stonewall, 830-644-2681; www.beckervineyards.com*
When San Antonio residents Richard Becker and his wife, Bunny, bought a log cabin just east of Fredericksburg in the Hill Country in the early '90s, the plan was simply to renovate. But being wine aficionados, they noticed some vineyard activity in the neighborhood and eventually planted two vineyards—one in 1992 and one in 1994. Next, of course, came the winery, located in a 19th-century German stone barn reproduction, surrounded by wildflowers and coastal Bermuda-grass fields, and a tasting room replete with a bar from an 1800s saloon imported from San Antonio. Vinos at the literally historic bar include chardonnay, grenache and cabernet/syrah combos, and our favorites: chenin blanc (fermented dry with pure fruit and excellent acidity), viognier (also the fuller, drier style similar to the Stags' Leaps from Napa Valley) and cabernet sauvignon reserve (a big, rich cabernet for your next steak). If the tasting turns out to be a full-day affair,

FLAT CREEK ESTATE

stay the night at the bed and breakfast on the property, The Homestead, a quaint and rustic log cabin. And if it's between April and June, you'll get the added bonus of waking up to the scent of the 10,000 blooming lavender flowers, red poppies and Texas blue bonnets that the Beckers planted across three acres in 1998.

Monday-Thursday 10 a.m.-5 p.m., Friday-Saturday 10 a.m.-6 p.m., Sunday noon-6 p.m.

### Fall Creek Vineyards

*1820 County Road 222, Tow, 325-379-5361; www.fcv.com*

You'll feel more like Alice in Wonderland than a visitor to tiny Tow, Texas, when you coast down the driveway through a 25-year-old grove of cyprus trees leading to the striking, white-stone winery at Fall Creek, located on beautiful Lake Buchanan. Susan and Ed Auler, pioneers and primary founders of the modern Texas wine industry, started Fall Creek in 1975 on a fourth-generation family ranch about 40 minutes north of Marble Falls. Starting with French-American hybrid vines in the mid '70s—most people then thought European vinifera vines like chardonnay and cabernet sauvignon would not be productive in the Hill Country—the Aulers soon switched to mostly European vinifera vines under the guidance of a top consultant in California, Andre Tchelistcheff, of B.V. Private Reserve Cabernet Sauvignon fame. Over the years, Fall Creek has garnered more than 500 local, national and international medals, with its sauvignon blanc, chardonnay, viognier (a relative newcomer to Texas), merlot, cabernet sauvignon and the meritus blend (possibly the best wine ever produced in Texas; Fall Creek's 2004 red is available in limited quantities now). Go for the wine but stay for the tour by Vanishing Texas River Cruise (www.vtrc.com), which takes you for a ride near the property's 90-foot waterfall.

Monday-Friday 11 a.m.-4 p.m., Saturday 11 a.m.-5 p.m., Sunday noon- 4 p.m.

TEXAS

### Flat Creek Estate
*24912 Singleton Bend East Road, Marble Falls, 512-267-6310; www.flatcreekestate.com*

Flat Creek Estate is nestled in the Texas Hill Country near the north shore of Lake Travis, about an hour from downtown Austin and 20 minutes east of Marble Falls. Founded by Rick and Madelyn Naber, the first vineyard was planted in 2000 and the winery was completed in 2001. In a remarkably short time, fame knocked on the door in the form of their 2003 Super Texan Sangiovese, which won a double gold medal in the San Francisco International Wine Competition. But don't just go for the Super Texan; other standouts include the pinot grigio, muscato and the Buckin' Horse Red (a blend comprised of cabernet sauvignon, syrah, sangiovese, primitivo and merlot). Tuesday-Friday and Sunday noon-5 p.m., Saturday 10 a.m.-5 p.m.

*Wildseed Farms ▪ Alamosa Wine Cellars ▪ The Driskill ▪ Mojitos at Fonda San Miguel*

## TWO-DAY ITINERARY

To get a taste of Texas Hill Country wineries, you only need two days and a designated driver.

**DAY 1:** Schedule a 10 a.m. tour and tasting at **Alamosa Wine Cellars** (see pg. 137); then head to **Fall Creek Vineyards** (left) at noon or 12:30 p.m. for a tasting and picnic lunch (on the way, you can pick up snacks at the **Bluffton Store** (*11635 Ranch Road 2241, 325-379-9837*). After that, take some time to shop in Marble Falls' darling boutiques, or go straight for the bottle and head to **Flat Creek Estate** (above) for a tour and tasting. Go back to Marble Falls for dinner and a good night's rest.

**DAY 2:** Drive to **Becker Vineyards** (see pg. 137) for a tour and tasting in the morning before lunching in Fredericksburg; then visit another local winery, like **Torre di Pietra Winery** (*10915 East Highway 290, 830-644-2829*). Save up your energy for **Mandola Estate Winery** (see pg. 140), where you should definitely take a tour and tasting at around 5p.m. and then get dinner at **Trattoria Lisina** (*512-894-3111*) next door.

PEACHES IN FREDERICKSBURG

TRIO RESTAURANT

**Mandola Estate Winery**
*13308 FM 150 W., Driftwood, 512-858-1470; www.mandolawines.com*
About 25 miles southwest of Austin, you will discover an imposing but elegant Tuscan-style winery and eatery. PBS celebrity chef Damian Mandola, co-founder of Carraba's and Damian's, "retired" five years ago and moved to Austin. Fast forward to 2006, when state-of-the-art winery, Mandola Estate Winery, popped up on a perfectly framed piece of property near tiny Driftwood. The finest winery restaurant in the state, Trattoria Lisina, followed a year later. With winemaker Mark Penna in place and Mandola at the helm, this breathtaking compound is already the talk of Hill Country. A substantial and diversified menu awaits you at Trattoria Lisina, and standout wines served at the Estate tasting room next door include pinot grigio, viognier (one of our favorites thanks to its lovely peach and apricot flavors), sangiovese, montepulciano, syrah and a lovely dessert wine. Upcoming

# FESTIVALS

Events and festivals abound in Hill Country. Among the best are the three-day **Chocolate Festival** in Austin (March); **Texas Hill Country Wine and Food Festival**, the area's oldest, largest and most acclaimed (April); the **Austin Wine Festival**, which comes with a side of great live music (May); the **Fredericksburg Wine and Food Fest** (October); and **New World Wine and Food Festival** in San Antonio (November).

If you're here in early April through early May, you'll also see a veritable explosion of Texas blue bonnets, Indian paintbrush and other vividly colored flowers blooming in full force. Be sure to visit the **Lady Bird Johnson Wildflower Center** *(512-292-4100; www.wildflower.org)*; **Wildseed Farms** near Fredericksburg, *(800-848-0078; www.wildseedfarms.com)*; and see the lavender and bluebonnets at **Becker Vineyards**.

## TOURS

Many of the wineries have their own tours, so call ahead to check for sign-up and availability.

### Austin Aloha Limousine
*512-458-5466, 877-693-0800; www.austinalohalimo.com*
Do it up Texas-style and take a customized wine tour with AAL, which boast the largest fleet of SUVs in the Hill Country region. You pick the wineries you want to visit, and a driver whisks you away to two to three vineyards (half-day tour) or four to six (full-day tour). They're strictly designated drivers, so don't expect much background information on the area, but at least you can tipple with a clear conscience.

### Texas Wine Tours
*877-839-9463, 830-997-8687; www.texas-wine-tours.com*
Hop on at Fredericksburg (or elsewhere for an additional charge), and this tour company will take care of your day in Hill Country, which includes shuttling you to five wineries and picking up the lunch tab at a local restaurant. Or keep it short and sweet with the Short Tour, which covers three wineries in the span of three hours.

### Wine Tasting Tours of Horseshoe Bay
*830-265-0044; www.hsbwinetours.com*
This tour company specializes in chauffeuring around small tour groups (two to six people) to the wineries of your choice in half- and full-day tours. Time permitting, tours end with a visit to a chocolate shop and a gourmet food store, though the tour includes a picnic lunch and plenty of water to keep you hydrated.

releases will include a slightly sweet moscato (with orange blossom and peach nuances), a dolcetto and a vermentino.
Monday 10 a.m.-6 p.m., Tuesday-Saturday 10 a.m.-10 p.m., Sunday 10 a.m.-9 p.m.

## STAY

### ★★★The Driskill
*604 Brazos St., Austin, 512-474-5911, 800-252-9367; www.driskillhotel.com*
The Driskill has been an Austin landmark since its opening in 1886. Experience the rich, dark ambience of the historic rooms in the original hotel or the fresh, light colors of the Texas Hill Country-inspired rooms in the adjacent 1929 tower. Pets get an experience all their own, with a custom bed, and gourmet treats and bottled water served in designer dishes. The Driskill Grill remains one of Austin's top restaurants.
189 rooms. Wireless Internet access. Two restaurants, two bars. Pets accepted. $$

THE MANSION AT JUDGES' HILL

#### ★★★★Four Seasons Hotel Austin
*98 San Jacinto Blvd., Austin, 512-478-4500, 800-819-5053; www.fourseasons.com/austin*
Set amid the rolling hills of Austin overlooking Lady Bird Lake, the elegant hotel maintains the integrity of the Four Seasons brand but also tips its hat to its Texas roots with touches such as cowhide-covered sofas in the lobby. Guest rooms feature cushy beds, plush terry robes and DVD players. Trio restaurant serves classics like steak and seafood with contemporary flair. Lose the guilt over the previous day's excess with a yoga class in the fitness center or a hike on the adjacent Lady Bird Lake Hike and Bike Trail. 291 rooms. Wireless Internet access. Restaurant, bar. Fitness center. Spa. Pool. Business center. $$$

#### ★★Hotel San José
*1316 S. Congress Ave., Austin, 512-444-7322, 800-574-8897; www.sanjosehotel.com*
Nestled on boho South Congress Avenue, this ultra-hip, revitalized classic—originally built in 1936 as a "modern tourist court," a.k.a., a motel—still retains much of its historic charm. From the '50s-era neon hotel sign outside and the mid-century modern-dominated décor peppered with Texas touches (like cowhide rugs and gardens with native plants) to an antique typewriter and Polaroid camera available at the front desk for artistically inclined guests, this boutique hotel is certainly in touch with its roots. Don't miss the rotating artwork from local artists, and do take advantage of the hotel's bike rental option and its extensive film and music library. And speaking of music: If you're in Austin for a music festival, make reservations well in advance—this place is a favorite for bands and musicians.
40 rooms. High-speed Internet access. Coffee shop, bar. Pool. Bike rental. $$

#### ★★★The Mansion At Judges' Hill
*1900 Rio Grande, Austin, 512-495-1800, 800-311-1619; www.judgeshill.com*
A grand structure built as a private home at the turn of the 20th century,

this boutique hotel retains its grandeur by filling the rooms with antiques from every period, canopied beds and original (though ornamental) fireplaces. The venue is popular with Austin brides and grooms, so get away from the hullaballoo in the lobby by ducking into the lounge and restaurant, which serve modern takes on classic recipes, such as roasted rack of lamb with mint risotto.

48 rooms. High-speed Internet access. Restaurant, bar. Pets accepted. $$$

### The Antlers Hotel

*1001 King St., Kingsland, 325-388-4411, 800-383-0007; www.theantlers.com*

Listed on the National Register of Historic Places, the Antlers Hotel is one quirky landmark. The old-time antique-filled hotel sits in the middle of 15 acres along Lake LBJ. More secluded rustic cabins are spread out near the waterfront, where guests can use the dock and boat slips or just take in the scenery from the porch of an 1870s log cabin. But the best places to stay on the grounds are the three converted caboose trains. Each brightly colored car has bunk beds, a small eating area, a couch, outdoor grills and picnic tables. For regional cuisine, stop by the hotel's Junction House, a quaint restaurant whose façade was featured in *The Texas Chainsaw Massacre*.

18 rooms. $$

### Horseshoe Bay Resort Marriott

*200 Hi Circle N., Horseshoe Bay, 830-598-8600, 866-799-5384; www.horseshoebaymarriott.com*

Horseshoe Bay seems more like an exclusive country club than a hotel. It boasts 12 tennis courts, a private beach and marina, four pools, two fitness centers and even a private airstrip. Duffers flock to the hotel to putt around on the property's three private championship golf courses. The rooms aren't too shabby, either, as their floor-to-ceiling windows offer a view of Lake LBJ or the lovely Hill Country.

349 rooms. High-speed Internet access. Three restaurants, two bars. Two fitness centers. Spa. $$

## EAT

### ★★★Driskill Grill

*604 Brazos St., Austin, 512-474-5911, 800-252-9367; www.driskillhotel.com*

Consistently named among Austin's top restaurants, the refined Driskill Grill changes up seafood and steakhouse fare with dishes such as cinnamon-dusted duck breast with savoy greens and apple-raisin hollandaise. It also offers a hefty wine list—you are in Texas' wine country, after all—with more than 450 selections. To see what goes on behind the stove at this award-winning restaurant, reserve the six-seat chef's table, located in the middle of the kitchen.

New American menu. Dinner. Reservations recommended. $$$

### ★★★Fonda San Miguel

*2330 W. North Loop, Austin, 512-459-4121; www.fondasanmiguel.com*

A pioneer in regional Mexican cooking, this hacienda has been famous for its food since the late '70s. Specialties include gulf shrimp with salsa verde, enchiladas suizas and traditional chicken mole. A superior wine list and a knockout brunch round out the experience. The restaurant also has earned a reputation for its vast collection of works from prominent Mexican artists such as Rufino Tamayo.

THE SPA AT FOUR SEASONS AUSTIN

Mexican menu. Dinner, Sunday brunch. Bar. Business casual attire. Reservations recommended. $$

### ★★★Hudson's on the Bend
*3509 Ranch Road 620 N., Austin, 512-266-1369; www.hudsonsonthebend.com*
Dining in Texas requires an adventurous spirit. Case in point: an appetizer of diamond-back rattlesnake cakes coiled on a pool of piquant chipotle cream. This is the kind of unusual cuisine found at this Hill Country eatery. Chefs Jeff Blank and Robert Rhoades serve up dishes such as pecan wood-smoked duck breast shingled with seared diver scallops in wild boar sweet potato hash, topped with blackberry chipotle sauce. The chefs then punctuate that experience with decadent desserts like caramel pecan pie dipped in Belgian chocolate.
Southwestern menu. Dinner. Bar. Casual attire. Reservations recommended. $$$

### ★★★Trio
*98 San Jacinto Blvd., Austin, 512-685-8300; www.fourseasons.com/austin*
The warm red and brown-hued dining room of Trio, nestled in the Four Seasons Austin, is quickly becoming a local favorite for its superlative Sunday brunch and for executive chef Elmar Prambs' fresh, seasonal, contemporary cuisine. At dinner, choose from dishes such as smoked Texas rib-eye or rice-flake-crusted halibut, before making a selection from the 300-plus bottles of wine, with 60 available by the glass.
New American menu. Breakfast, lunch, dinner, Sunday brunch. Reservations recommended. $$$

### South Congress Café
*1600 S. Congress Ave., Austin, 512-447-3905; www.southcongresscafe.com*
Is it a bar? Is it a restaurant? With crabcakes this good, who cares? In this laid-back but space age-looking spot, worlds collide (in a very good way). Fashionistas mingle with scruffy musicians and too-cool hipsters, all drawn in by outstanding dishes, like eggs benedict with chipotle sauce and beef

TEXAS

tenderloin over horseradish-spiked hash. Wrap up dinner—or the famously popular brunch—with the signature Trudy's Mexican Martini, but be warned: it's so deliciously potent, you may never figure out how to classify the place. American, Southwestern menu. Brunch, happy hour, dinner. $$$

### Trattoria Lisina
*13308 FM 150 W., Driftwood, 512-894-3111; www.trattorialisina.com*
When you see Mandola Estate Winery's Trattoria Lisina, you'll wonder if you're at the right place. The stone restaurant looks more like a Tuscan villa than a mere trattoria. And with acclaimed chef Damian Mandola—host of the PBS cooking show *Cucina Sicilia*, author of the unequivocally Texan-sounding cookbook *Ciao Y'All* and co-founder of the Carrabba's Italian Grill empire—at the helm, Lisina elevates traditional trattoria fare. Specialties include Anatra all'Arancio (roasted duck with orange sauce) and Osso Bucco. Order up a bottle of Mandola's fine vino to pair with your meal.
Italian menu. Lunch, dinner. $$$

*The Mansion at Judges' Hill • Trio Restaurant • LakeHouse Spa at Lake Austin Spa Resort • Horseshoe Bay Resort by Marriot*

## SPA

### ★★★★The Spa at Four Seasons Austin
*98 San Jacinto Blvd., Austin, 512-685-8300; www.fourseasons.com/austin*
This spa inside the Four Seasons Austin offers a full range of pampering treatments, including wraps, massages, facials and pedicures. Signature services include the Lavender-Lemongrass Journey, which begins with a lavender sea salt scrub, followed by a lavender-lemongrass body butter wrap and concludes with a head-to-toe massage. The men's treatment menu includes a natural spice body buff and a manicure complete with a hand massage.

### LakeHouse Spa at Lake Austin Spa Resort
*1705 Quinlan Park Road, Austin, 512-372-7300, 800-847-5637; www.lakeaustin.com*
This 25,000-square-foot retreat offers more than 100 services. Opt for something different, like the Manaka Tapping Treatment, an ancient practice to relax and invigorate your body in which your accupoints are lightly tapped with a wooden hammer and peg. But you can't go wrong

SOUTH CONGRESS AVENUE SHOPPING

FOUR SEASONS AUSTIN

with Olive Our Love. The signature treatment uses the antioxidant-rich fruit for an exfoliating scrub of ground olive stones, and warm olive oil moisturizes you while you're cocooned in a wrap. After an olive oil scalp massage, the rest of your body gets kneaded.

## SHOP

### South Congress Avenue Shopping
*South Congress Avenue, Riverside to Oltorf Street, Austin*
Forget mainstream malls and check out the shopping area nicknamed "SoCo." One-of-a-kind stores with names like Lucy in Disguise with Diamonds, New Bohemia and Uncommon Objects sell everything from vintage clothes and kitschy antiques to 1950s furniture, Mexican imports and more.

## SEE AND DO

### Austin Museum of Art
*823 Congress Ave., Austin, 512-495-9224; www.amoa.org*
Modern and contemporary American art exhibits swing by AMOA's downtown location (the original museum is in Laguna Gloria) regularly, such as a recent show featuring the work of Sol LeWitt. The museum pays homage to its state through its permanent collection, which includes both contemporary and classic works by Texas artists. Tuesday-Saturday 10 a.m.-6 p.m. (until 8 p.m. on Thursday), Sunday noon-5 p.m.; closed Monday.

### Sixth Street
*Southeast of the Capitol Complex on Sixth Street between Congress Avenue and I-35, Austin, 512-974-2000; www.6street.com*
Home of the rocking South by Southwest Festival, Austin bills itself as the "Live Music Capital of the World." In this entertainment district, sometimes compared to New Orleans' Bourbon Street, you'll hear everything from rock and hip-hop to soul and jazz in the many bars and nightclubs.

# CHAPTER 9
# VIRGINIA
# MONTICELLO WINE TRAIL

Boars Head Inn ▪ Dinner at Palladio ▪ Sunset at the Mark Addy ▪ Inn at Little Washington

Thomas Jefferson would be proud if he were alive today. The former president loved wines and tried for 30 years to cultivate foreign vines in the soil of his home state of Virginia. His efforts were unsuccessful due to a pesky insect called the phylloxera louse, which decimated the roots of the European varietals. It wasn't until decades later that farmers solved the problem by grafting European vines to the heartier roots of American grapevines. Through grafting, the development of modern pesticides and a renewed interest in wines in the latter half of the 20th century, Jefferson's dream became reality.

There are now more than 250 vineyards and 100 wineries in Virginia, with 21 clustered around Jefferson's hometown of Charlottesville on what's called the Monticello Wine Trail. Each winery on this trail has a unique history, a beautiful setting, a tasting room, tours and a wide assortment of wines. Even a vinophile such as Jefferson would have a hard time sampling the bounty from all the different stops on the trail, so here are eight excellent examples that deliver a truly Jeffersonian experience.

For more information on the Montecello Wine Trail and a complete listing of vineyards, vist www.monticellowinetrail.org. For all Virginia wines, visit www.virginiawines.org.

BARBOURSVILLE VINEYARDS

# TASTE
### Afton Mountain
*234 Vineyard Lane, Afton, 540-456-8667; www.aftonmountainvineyards.com*
With its first planting in 1978, Afton Mountain is one of the oldest of the modern wineries in the state. Though it does use contemporary filtering and testing equipment, Afton tries to rely on ancient farming techniques. They don't use herbicides or irrigation, and they hand-harvest all of the grapes. To eliminate damage to the fruit and juice, they utilize a gravity-flow system, instead of pumps, to allow the grapes to flow naturally during processing. With these old-world techniques, the winemakers strive to produce crisp, subtle and delicate wines. Wines include chardonnay, riesling, cabernet franc, cabernet sauvignon and a couple of varieties usually not grown in Virginia, gewürztraminer, pinot noir and sangiovese. Their sparkling wine, Tête de Cuvée, utilizes the traditional French méthode champenoise, where the bubbles, for the bubbly, are produced during a second fermentation within the bottle. Be sure to sample the Old Vine Cabernet Sauvignon—it's as smooth as cream.
March-December, Wednesday-Monday 10 a.m-6 p.m. (10 a.m.-5 p.m. November-December); January-February, Friday-Monday 11 a.m.-5 p.m., or by apppointment.

### Barboursville Vineyards
*17655 Winery Road, Barboursville, 540-832-3824; www.barboursvillewine.com*
Founded in 1976, Barboursville is more than just an impressive winery with a portfolio of at least 16 different varietals. It's a destination with a beautiful inn and a wonderful restaurant, Palladio. The sumptuous estate houses the ruins of the Barbour family home, one of only three houses designed for friends by Thomas Jefferson. The 1814 structure, which burned in 1884, was centered around a three-story octagonal edifice that included a grand two-story main room. The impressive ruins still stand overlooking a historic countryside that has generated a new history in the production of fine wines. Winemaker Luca Paschina crafts the wines by carefully selecting the perfect patch of land for each variety and planting, harvesting and oversee-

VERITAS WINERY

ing every step of production. A standout bottle is the Nebbiolo Reserve, which is made entirely from nebbiolo, a grape from the Piedmont region of Italy. The wine is barrel-aged for one year and then bottle-aged for another before release. It has the intensity desired by anyone who dreams of a complex, full-bodied wine.

Monday-Saturday 10 a.m.-5 p.m., Sunday 11 a.m.-5 p.m. Free tours of winery Saturday-Sunday at noon, 4 p.m., and by appointment.

### First Colony

*1650 Harris Creek Road, Charlottesville, 434-979-7105;*
*www.firstcolonywinery.com*

First Colony is proof that if you have a passion for grapes and a little help from some pros, you can make great wines. Owner Randolph McElroy, Jr. (Randy) worked in construction for 20 years before indulging his dream of owning a winery. With the help of viticulturists and winemakers, he started making wine under the First Colony name in 2002. The winery produces three whites, six reds, a rosé, a claret and two dessert wines. For a bit of whimsy, try the Sweet Shanando. This agreeable white is named after the original spelling of Shenandoah and includes a whopping four percent residual sugar. For an unusual red, indulge your senses with the award-winning tannat. It's a blend of 85 percent tannat (a grape from the Pyrenees) and fifteen percent touriga, the most notable grape of Portugal. These two unusual varieties come together to form deep purple wine with the richness of ripe plums.

Monday-Friday 9 a.m.-5 p.m., Saturday 11 a.m.-5 p.m.

### Jefferson Vineyards

*1353 Thomas Jefferson Parkway, Charlottesville, 434-977-3042;*
*www.jeffersonvineyards.com*

The land originally chosen by Thomas Jefferson and Italian Fillipo Mazzei to start a vineyard in 1774 is now home to Jefferson Vineyards. Planted in 1981, the vineyard has produced award-winning wines for more than 20 years and is now led by winemaker Andy Reagan. Andy began working in vineyards at age 18 (not even legal drinking age) in Upstate New York at

VIRGINIA

Benmarl Vineyards. He became head winemaker there after a few years and then worked as the winemaker at several Virginia wineries before settling down at Jefferson. His wines include Jefferson's Own Vin Blanc, a blend of chardonnay, viognier and vidal blanc, and the international gold medal-winning Meritage. A mix of cabernet franc, merlot, petit verdot and cabernet sauvignon, this Bordeaux-style blend has rich flavors suggesting coffee and chocolate. Inhale deeply to savor the full complexity of a wine made from so many different grapes.
Daily 10 a.m.-6 p.m.

## Keswick Vineyards

*1575 Keswick Winery Drive, Keswick, 434-244-3341; www.keswickvineyards.com*
A relative newcomer, Keswick opened in 2002 with a splash. Its first vintage garnered 38 awards, including Best White Wine in America at the Atlanta International Wine Summit. While still a young winery (the tasting room opened in 2006) Keswick is steeped in history. The 400-acre farm on Edgewood Estate was instrumental in both the Revolutionary and Civil Wars. During the Civil War, more than 10,000 Confederate troops camped on the

*Keswick Vineyards • Keswick Hall Exterior • Pool at Keswick Hall • Garden Fountain at Mark Addy*

grounds around the estate. And during the Revolution, British soldiers were delayed at Edgewood (the landowner, Dr. Thomas Walker, asked the troops to stay for breakfast to slow down their advance), allowing Thomas Jefferson and the Virginia Legislation to escape the region in 1781. So why not enjoy a little wine for breakfast to commemorate this feat? The 2006 Norton wine, made from a native grape, is as black as coffee and tastes of plums and black cherries. White wine lovers should try the Verdejo, a Spanish grape mixed with seven percent viognier to produce a light, aromatic wine with the fruity flavors of green apples and pears.
Daily 9 a.m.- 5 p.m.

## Prince Michel

*154 Winery Lane, Leon, 540-547-3707, 800-800-9463; www.princemichel.com*
Prince Michel is the northernmost winery on the Monticello Wine Trail and also one of the oldest wineries in the state. For more than 25 years, the vineyard has been an easy pit stop for thirsty travelers driving south to Charlottesville on Route 29—you can pull into and out of the winery parking lot like a highway rest stop. The winery features self-guided tours of the barrel room and production facilities and a spacious tasting room

overlooking the stainless steel fermentation tanks and barrels. The winery produces numerous wines, including a sparkling wine and a port. It offers the usual assortment of well-known varietals, including chardonnay, riesling, pinot grigio, cabernet sauvignon, cabernet franc and merlot. There's also a shiraz for those who love a hearty red and the Très Bien, a dessert wine with honey and apricot notes made from the rare petit manseng grape.
January-March, Monday-Thursday 10 a.m.-5 p.m., Friday-Sunday 10 a.m.-6 p.m., April-December, daily 10 a.m.-6 p.m.

### Veritas Winery
*145 Saddleback Farm, Afton, 540-456-8000; www.veritaswines.com*
As a popular stop on Virginia Wine Country tours, with easy access from Interstate 64, Veritas is always buzzing. Don't be discouraged if the parking lot is full. The grand tasting room and long bar are big enough to fit large groups of people. Established in 2002 by Andrew and Patricia Hodson, this family-run vineyard is complemented by daughter Emily, who holds a master's degree in oenology. Emily crafted the 2005 Kenmar, a traminette that won the 2007 National Women's Wine Competition. For a taste of something different, try the petit manseng. This grape from Southwestern France produces a perfect white wine for hot summer days and delivers flavors reminiscent of tropical fruits, with a hint of piña colada. Grab a bottle and kick back with a glass on the sunny deck overlooking the Blue Ridge Mountains.
Monday-Friday 9:30 a.m.-5:30 p.m., Saturday-Sunday 11 a.m.-5 p.m.

### Wintergreen Winery
*462 Winery Lane, Nellysford, 404-361-2519; www.wintergreen-winery.com*
Situated at the foot of a resort bearing the same name, Wintergreen offers some of the highest quality, least expensive wines in the state. Several are priced under $15. The cozy tasting room and shop are located in a 19th-century farm building surrounded by green rolling hills, farms, pastures and mountains. The Three Ridges White is a blend of the Spanish grape verdejo and chardonnay that combine to make a unique dry, white wine with an apricot bouquet. The Three Ridges Red mixes

MONTICELLO

HUNT CLUB AT BOARS HEAD INN

chambourcin and cabernet franc for a hearty full-bodied red that's perfect for cold nights in the mountains. The winery also produces a merlot, several chardonnays and a viognier, a hard-to-grow French grape that thrives in the Blue Ridge foothills. Rounding out the selection are apple and raspberry fruit wines. Neither is too syrupy and both work well chilled and served with desserts. Daily April-October 10 a.m. to 6 p.m., November-March 10 a.m. to 5 p.m.

## STAY

### ★★★Boar's Head Inn
*200 Ednam Drive, Charlottesville, 434-296-2181; www.boarsheadinn.com*
Named after a famed British inn, this grand resort with 159 rooms and 11 suites retains the charm of a small country lodging. Rooms feature beamed ceilings, four-poster beds, antiques, mahogany desks and marble washstands, and many have balconies overlooking the 573-acre estate. The heart of the resort is an 1834 gristmill that was painstakingly disassembled and rebuilt at the inn's present location. The property also has an 18-hole golf course, four restaurants, three swimming pools and a 5,000-square-foot spa.
170 rooms. Four restaurants, bar. Spa. Pool. Golf. $$$

### ★★★★★Inn at Little Washington
*309 Main St., Washington, 540-675-3800; www.theinnatlittlewashington.com*
The unassuming exterior of this little inn (which is housed in a building that was once a gas station) reveals nothing of the quiet luxury you'll find inside. The inn was decorated by London stage set designer Joyce Evans in collaboration with the inn's owner and chef, Patrick O'Connell, using a style that could be described as eclectic English country. Bedrooms are swathed in chintzes and toiles and stocked with impressive antique beds and chairs, while public spaces are filled with cozy, inviting settees. Whatever style you call it, the interior is inviting. The inn has 18 rooms and suites, each uniquely decorated, plus two separate cottages. The well-trained staff is ready to take care of any and all needs—from packing a picnic to drawing out a route for a scenic drive, to making reservations for any activity or being available to serve tea or wine if you wish to do nothing at all.
18 rooms. Closed Tuesday in January-March and July. Complimentary continental breakfast. Restaurant, bar. $$$$

### ★★★Keswick Hall
*701 Club Drive, Keswick, 434-979-3440; www.keswick.com*
Relax in one of 48 rooms and suites at this sprawling, luxurious estate located near Thomas Jefferson's home of Monticello. Each individually decorated space is furnished with American and English antiques and swathed in fresh, pretty toiles, chintzes and plaids. Amenities include CD players, clawfoot tubs and welcome baskets with locally made treats. The luxury hotel sits on more than 600 acres of countryside and includes an Arnold Palmer Signature 18-hole golf course, two restaurants, two bars, a swimming pool and a spa. Go for the wine-inspired signature treatment called the Vinotherapy, which utilizes red grape components from the vine to the seed to instill the body and face with antioxidants and anti-aging

PORCH AT THE INN AT LITTLE WASHINGTON

polyphenois. In-room massage is also available.
48 rooms. Two restaurants, two bars. Spa. Pool. Golf. $$$

### ★★★Wintergreen Resort
*Route 664, Wintergreen, 434-325-2200; www.wintergreenresort.com*
With just about every outdoor activity you can think of (golfing, skiing, biking, hiking, and swimming, to name a few) and four restaurants, this resort has it all. A variety of accommodations is available including rooms at the lodge, one- to three-bedroom condos and houses with up to nine bedrooms. Abutting the Blue Ridge Parkway, Wintergreen shines as an environmentally friendly resort. When it was first designed, developers set aside 6,000 acres of the 11,000-acre property to remain as wilderness. And at an elevation of nearly 4,000 feet, this green resort offers cool temperatures and amazing sunrise views. Check out the special outdoor and adventure packages.
300 rooms. Ski in/ski out. Restaurant, bar. $$

### 1804 Inn
*17655 Winery Road, Barboursville, 434-760-2212; www.barboursvillewine.com*
This inn, located at Barboursville Vineyards and housed on the grounds of an estate designed by Thomas Jefferson, has three sumptuous suites and a separate cottage, each with a working fireplace. Two of the suites (Octagon and Malvaxia) feature a 45-foot-long, southern-facing balcony with views of the lake, mountains and vineyards, plus a northern balcony at garden level and a private garden and lawn. The third suite, Philéo, includes a secluded and covered brick garden-level terrace and a magnificent terrace with inviting Adirondack chaises that are ideal for relaxing the afternoon away. The Cottage, the former 18th-century brick servants' quarters, features wood beam ceilings, slate floors and two individual suites. It's perfect for couples traveling together.
4 rooms. Complimentary breakfast. $$$

FOSSETT'S RESTAURANT

### Inn at Monticello
*1188 Scottsville Road, Charlottesville, 434-979-3593; www.innatmonticello.com*
Only one mile from Monticello, this bed and breakfast sits on five acres of land in an alluring valley with mountain views and trees filled with songbirds. The English-style house in which the inn is located dates back to the mid-1800s and includes five rooms and a separate cottage suite. Rooms are decorated with oriental rugs on hardwood floors and traditional furnishings. Two of the upstairs rooms have wood-burning fireplaces and the cottage includes a gas-burning one. The two downstairs rooms open to sitting porches. A Wine Dinner Getaway includes two nights' accommodations, gourmet breakfasts, a welcome glass of wine, dinner at a local restaurant, a guide to area wineries, two wine glasses and, of course, a bottle of local vino.
5 rooms. High-speed Internet access. Complimentary full breakfast. $$

### The Mark Addy
*56 Rodes Farm Drive, Nellysford, 434-361-1101; www.mark-addy.com*
Located in the foothills of the Blue Ridge Mountains and close to Veritas, Wintergreen and Afton vineyards, this country bed and breakfast features wide porches and balconies, and 10 individually decorated guest rooms. For the full wine-weekend experience, try the Wine Lovers Scavenger Hunt. Scour the countryside seeking out clues while touring at least four vineyards—The package includes a two-night stay, breakfasts each morning, two bottles of wine and a prize for finding all of the clues. Or try the all-inclusive package, which offers accommodations, breakfast, a picnic lunch and three-course dinner daily, snacks and a bottle of wine each day.
10 rooms. Restaurant. $$

### The White Pig
*5120 Irish Road, Schuyler, 434-831-1416; www.thewhitepig.com*
This beautifully restored 1906 Victorian farmhouse is a bed and breakfast with a twist: all the food served here is vegan. The inn sits on more than 170 acres and includes an animal sanctuary with a dozen rescued pot belly pigs. Each of the four rooms at the inn offers a view of the forest and

meadows on the farm. The most popular room, the Jacob, features a large picture window that gives the impression of sleeping out in the wilderness, even though the room has a luxurious king-sized bed resting on an elegantly carved cherry frame.
4 rooms. Complimentary breakfast. $$

# EAT

## ★★C&O
*515 E. Water St., Charlottesville, 434-971-7044; www.candorestaurant.com*
Behind the simple brick façade of this downtown restaurant (which once housed a railway diner), upscale American cooking is served in six distinctive eating areas: a barside bistro, a mezzanine with plank floors and wood-burning stove, a light and airy upstairs featuring high ceilings and exposed wooden beams, a covered and heated outdoor patio, an open terrace where you can enjoy a starry night, and a gallery perfect for private functions. No matter which room you choose, you are assured a meal featuring the freshest ingredients from a seasonal menu designed by chef Thomas Bowles. Dishes might include beef tenderloin with bordelaise sauce and barley grits, or rainbow trout baked in a salt crust.
American menu. Dinner. $$

## ★★★Fossett's at Keswick Hall
*701 Club Drive, Keswick, 434-979-3440; www.keswick.com*
This restaurant delivers a meal with a view. Floor-to-ceiling windows on three sides of this hotel dining room provide a brilliant panoramic peek at the rolling green hills and the Southwest Mountains, a range that parallels the Blue Ridge Mountains. American country cuisine is created by a culinary team led by executive chef Craig Hartman, who trained at the Culinary Institute of America, was a two-time guest chef at New York's celebrated James Beard House and performed on the World Champion United States Team at the Culinary Olympics.
American menu. Dinner, brunch. Jackets recommended, no jeans. $$

## ★★★★★The Inn at Little Washington
*309 Main St., Washington, 540-675-3800; www.theinnatlittlewashington.com*
This country inn is perhaps most famous for its restaurant. Chef Patrick O'Connell prepares seasonal dishes such as pecan-crusted soft shell crab tempura with compressed watermelon and Italian mustard fruit, or crispy sweetbreads with local grilled peaches, chanterelles and country ham. For dessert, there are temptations like pistachio and white chocolate ice cream terrine with blackberry sauce. And while the food is superlative, the service here is like nowhere else. Affable and attentive, the waitstaff expertly guides diners through their meals with the sole mission of delivering an unforgettable experience.
American menu. Dinner. Closed occasional Tuesdays (call ahead). Bar. Business casual attire. Reservations recommended. Valet parking. $$$$

## ★★Ivy Inn
*2244 Old Ivy Road, Charlottesville, 434-977-1222; www.ivyinnrestaurant.com*
This 200-year-old house has been converted into a unique restaurant where every space is given over to fine dining, from the living room to the three upstairs bedrooms. Chef and owner Angelo Vangelopoulos

prepares a new menu each day to make the most of fresh ingredients from local sources. The menu of regional Amerian cuisine includes dishes such as pumpkin seed-crusted wild Chesapeake rockfish fillet. Be sure to sample the bread, which is baked fresh at the inn's bakeshop.
American menu. Dinner. Closed Sunday. $$

### ★★★Old Mill Room at the Boars Head Inn
*200 Ednam Drive, Charlottesville, 434-972-2230; www.boarsheadinn.com*
This fine dining room serves classic dishes with an international twist. Different spices, used in recipes from around the world, are featured each month. You'll find unexpected and flavor-packed dishes like Moroccan-seared chicken with apricot couscous alongside pub standards such as lobster bisque and grilled filet mignon. Friendly service adds to the relaxed, old English tavern atmosphere.
International menu. Lunch, dinner, brunch. Jackets recommended at dinner. $$

*Vineyards • Guest Room at Kewsick Inn • Lunch at Fossett's Restaurant • Bistro at the Boars Head Inn*

### Bavarian Chef
*Route 29 South, Shelby, 540-948-6505*
This authentic German restaurant serves a sausage sampler with bratwurst, weisswurst and bauerwurst. The family-style eatery also serves large portions of sauerbraten, wienerschnitzel and, of course, German beer for when you're ready for a break from wine. Save room for dessert—the dessert tray is stocked full of tempting German treats such as apfelstrudel, Black Forest cake and German chocolate cake.
German menu. Dinner. $

### Fountain Room at the Mark Addy
*56 Rodes Farm Drive, Nellysford, 434-361-1101; www.mark-addy.com*
Unlike eateries at many inns, the Fountain Room at the Mark Addy is a full-service restaurant that serves dinner to those not staying onsite. The four-course menu changes daily and features dishes accented with herbs and produce grown in the restaurant's garden. Live music by top local musicians is performed on Saturday nights. A separate summer bistro menu includes three courses featuring continental and American cuisine for less than $20.

American menu. Dinner. Closed Sunday-Monday. Reservations recommended. $$

### L'Etoile
*817 W. Main St., Charlottesville, 434-979-7957; www.letoilerestaurant.com*
The French-inspired cuisine served at this sweet bistro relies heavily on game punctuated with a bit of Southern flare. Think pheasant with grits, venison and a side of sweet potato gnocchi, or duck with roasted root vegetables and a cider reduction. Desserts are rich and satisfying, from classic crème brulée to chocolate mocha pot du crème. The restaurant includes three upstairs dining rooms and a downstairs bistro.
Bistro menu. Lunch, dinner. $$

### Palladio Restaurant at Barbousville
*17655 Winery Road, Barbousville, 540-832-7848; www.barboursvillewine.com*
The Northern Italian gastronomical feasts served at this cozy restaurant are enhanced by the use of local seafood and produce. Traditional favorites such as risotto, ravioli, gnocchi and spaghetti take on new meanings when combined with local goat cheese, sautéed snails or artichokes in basil broth. Both lunch and dinner include an appetizer, first and second course and dessert. Each course includes a different Barbousville wine to complement the food.
Italian menu. Lunch, dinner. Jackets required at dinner. Reservations required. $$

## SHOP

### And George
*3466 Ivy Road, Charlottesville, 434-244-2800; www.andgeorge.com*
Founded by a mother and daughter team, this funky shop features an eclectic mix of handmade gifts, apothecary items, custom furniture, avant-garde clothing and antiques from around the country and around the world. Go often and be delighted each time you visit at the rare oddities and well-appointed pieces you'll find here.
Monday-Saturday 10 a.m.-5 p.m.

BARBOURSVILLE VINEYARDS

THE INN AT LITTLE WASHINGTON

VIRGINIA

### Basic Necessities
*2226 Rockfish Valley Highway (Route 151), Nellysford, 434-361-1766; www.basicnecessities.us*
This humble roadside shop sells imported cheeses, freshly baked breads, fine wines from around the world, gourmet coffees and teas, salsas, in-season vegetables and fine chocolates. Locally grown organic produce is spotlighted in the lunch, dinner and Sunday brunch that is served here. Tuesday-Sunday. Hours vary.

### Fermentation Trap
*6420 Seminole Trail, Barboursville, 434-985-2192; www.fermentationtrap.com*
If traveling through wine country inspires you to start making your own wine, the Fermentation Trap sells everything you'll need to get started, from wine starter kits to barrels to bottles and corks. If vino is not your niche, there are also kits and equipment for brewing beer.
Tuesday, Thursday-Friday 4-8 p.m., Saturday 10 a.m.-6 p.m., Sunday noon-5 p.m.

## WINE EVENTS

### First Colony Winery: Spring Open House
Celebrate the rites of spring with hors d'oeuvres, wine tastings, barrel samples, tours and new wine releases.
Free. First Saturday in April, noon-5 p.m.

### Barboursville Vineyards: Annual Autumn Explosion and Barrel Tasting
This event is an opportunity to buy rare vintages of Barboursville wines while listening to live music and sampling nibbles from Palladio Restaurant. $15 per person includes souvenir wine glass. First weekend in October, 11 a.m.-4 p.m.

### First Colony Winery: Interactive Cooking Class
Learn to cook from a guest chef. This class includes interactive cooking instruction, a four- or five-course meal, wine pairings, a tour, a tasting and a signature wine glass. $65 per person. Reservations required. First Sunday of each month, October-December, 11 a.m.–2 p.m. Dates vary so call ahead.

### Veritas: Starry Night Summer Concerts
Enjoy wine, live music and food under the stars. The entry fee of $10 per person includes a Veritas glass. Bring a picnic or purchase dinner, prepared by chef Said Rhafiri, for an additional $15. Reservation required for pre-made dinner. Second Saturday of each month, June-September, 7-11 p.m.

BARBOURSVILLE VINEYARDS

### Monticello Museum Shop
*931 Thomas Jefferson Parkway, Charlottesville, 434-984-9822; www.monticello.org*
This shop offers books on Thomas Jefferson and Monticello, as well as Jefferson collectibles, such as cups, unique wooden toys and porcelain dolls. There are also curios like kaleidoscopes and Lewis and Clark souvenirs.
March-October 9 a.m.-6 p.m., November-February 9 a.m.-5 p.m.

### The Odd Chest
*107 Martinsburg Ave., Gordonsville, 888-832-9050; www.theoddchest.com*
Take home a bit of the English Midlands at the Odd Chest. This antique store specializes in elegant English furniture solidly built of oak, mahogany, walnut and yew, with many pieces accented by intricate carvings, inlays and marble.
Monday-Tuesday, Thursday-Saturday 10 a.m.-6 p.m.

### Rockfish Gap Country Store
*8860 Rockfish Gap Turnpike, Afton, 540-456-6112;*
*www.rockfishgapcountrystore.com*
For more than 40 years this old-fashioned country store has sold handcrafted jewelry, glassware, local artwork, candies, quilts, toys, groceries and, of course, Virginia wines. A Christmas room features ornaments and decorations year round.
Daily 10 a.m.-5 p.m.

## CHAPTER 10
# WINE UNFILTERED

If you want to learn to sip like a sommelier, it's a good thing you're heading to wine country somewhere. The best way to learn about wine is to taste it—and taste it some more. Of course, when you get there, you'll hear people talking about tannins and legs (not the human kind) and using other wine lingo with which you may be already vaguely familiar.

This isn't chemistry class—so relax. You may not be Robert Parker (who, in case you don't already know, writes about wine) or have a subscription to *Wine Spectator* but you're no novice either. You know a good pinot noir when you taste it. Here's a primer, or a refresher, depending on your level of expertise, on the nitty gritty wine details, to ensure you have the best experience possible—because in the end, that's what counts. Here's to many educational—and fun—trips.

WINE UNFILTERED

## A LAY OF THE LAND

Wine tastings can range from classroom-like atmospheres to ones that feel like a chic cocktail party. Expect to encounter all levels of wine enthusiasts at either. The person behind the bar (often called the greeter) should explain tasting fees and the day's menu, which outlines the wines available for sample and purchase, and gives descriptions of the flavors found in each vintage. This will help you keep straight which wine is which (especially after a few heavy pours), and which bottles you might like to take home. If the tasting room doesn't have a menu, your greeter will describe them as you go along. Several wineries offer both a standard and a reserve tasting, so for a slightly higher price you can try some of the higher-end wines. Split both tastings with a friend for a chance to try everything.

Wine tasting fees can range from free to more than $45, although the average runs around $5 per person and often includes a complimentary wine glass imprinted with the vineyard's logo. Fees are usually waived if wine is purchased or if you join the wine club. Although you're not expected to tip, gratuity is certainly appreciated, so go ahead and leave a few benjamins if your greeter is especially helpful and friendly. Keep in mind that some wineries require reservations.

## WINE NOTES:

- Because heavier and sweeter wines can overpower their lighter counterparts, whites are tasted first, followed by reds and then dessert wines. Feel free to skip pours here and there, or stick to just reds or just whites. You could even pick a particular varietal to explore.

- Most wineries are used to two people sharing a glass and paying only one fee and will ask how many tastings you'd like.

- If water is provided, use it to clear your palate between wines or to clean your glass. Sometimes neutral food such as crackers or bread is also provided for palate cleansing.

- Use the spit bucket. You don't have to empty your glass every time you taste. If you don't like something or have had enough, use the bucket to simply pour out the remaining contents of your glass. This can be a good way to pace yourself if you're planning to visit several tasting rooms in one day.

- Ask your greeter about other vineyards in the area. This is often the best way to discover little-known gems or off the-beaten path wineries.

- Don't feel like you have to buy every bottle you sample. Be selective with your purchases—that's the whole point of getting to taste it first. Ask about shipping services if you decide to buy more than a few bottles—most airlines will not allow you to carry wine on board now that liquids are banned from the cabin.

- Many wineries offer attractive outdoor spots where you can picnic or simply relax, taking in the bucolic scenery. Attend the tasting first and perhaps pick up a bottle to pair with your meal. (Usually the winery will lend you glasses and a bottle opener.)

# SWIRL IT, SNIFF IT, SIP IT

## A FEW SIMPLE TIPS THAT WILL HAVE YOU SWILLING LIKE A CONNOISSEUR

First, pick up the glass and look at the wine. Hold it up to the light if you like, or against a plain white or light colored background, taking note of the color and clarity. Color best indicates the age of a wine. For instance, reds that appear purpler are indicative of a younger wine and those that appear darker red tend to be older. Whites that are green-hued hint at youth, while deeper yellows suggest older vintages.

**2** Hold the glass by the stem. Wine is served in stem glasses because the temperature at which it is served can greatly impact the taste; holding the glass by the stem enables you to avoid heating the wine with the palm of your hand.

**3** Swirl the glass using a firm wrist motion. Most people use their whole arm but the trick is really in the wrist. This motion releases the wine's aroma to the top of the glass. The swirling motion also aerates the wine itself, opening the flavor and intensity.

**4** After swirling, notice the wine's "legs." These are the rivulets that run down the sides of the glass and are telling of the body of a wine. Full-bodied wines are heavier and thus, come down the side of the glass in sheets. Medium-bodied wines are less thick and come down in rivulets (legs) and lighter wines do not hold to the sides of the glass when swirled.

**5** Hold your nose just over the rim of the glass and deeply inhale through your nostrils to get a sense of the wine's bouquet. Some common aromas to look for are apples (chardonnay), black cherry (pinot noir), cloves (bordeaux) and black pepper (syrah, grenache).

**6** Take your first sip. There are several ways to enhance the flavor of the wine as you drink it. One is to gently roll the wine over your tongue or swish it around your mouth before swallowing—this allows you to note the texture of the wine as well as let it really saturate your taste buds. Another tip is to hold a small amount of wine in your mouth while drawing in air through your lip—this one is a little tricky so you might want to practice with some water first. By doing this you are aerating the wine and emboldening the flavor.

**7** Read over the ingredients in the tasting notes and see if you can identify any of the flavors as you sip. Feel free to ask lots of questions and to even take notes. Most important, don't feel compelled to do any of the above. If a simple sip works for you, then stick with that.

SCHRAMSBERG VINEYARDS

## BUYING BOTTLES

Purchasing wines directly from a vineyard can be a great way to add fantastic bottles to your racks. You're getting a chance to sample the goods and make an informed shopping decision, and you're also more likely to come across reserve bottles or limited edition wines that you wouldn't be able to find elsewhere. A few things to consider before purchasing:

- Just because you did a tasting doesn't mean you have to purchase the wine.
- Buying wine by the caseload is often cheaper.
- Consider where you're going to store your wine purchases before heading home. High temperatures can ruin a bottle quickly, so if it's going to be heating up in your car trunk all day, bring along an insulated cooler.
- Joining a wine club (see box to the right) or signing up on a vineyard's mailing list will allow you to receive discounts and notification of special sales. Often wineries with large inventories discount their bottles to make room for the next vintage. Shipping costs vary state to state and make sure that you live in a state where alcohol can be delivered via the postal system.

## DO'S AND DON'TS

- Don't wear heavy perfume or cologne. This might interfere with your ability to enjoy the wine's aromas.
- Do take your time tasting the wine—there's no rush.
- Don't ask for a second pour unless it's a wine you're really considering buying.
- Don't volunteer your opinion of the wine until other tasters in your party have had a chance to sample—everyone's taste is different.
- Do keep it down! Even if a tasting room looks like a swanky bar, it isn't; getting overly loud or raucous is frowned upon. Most tasting rooms won't serve you if you appear too intoxicated.

## WINE CLUBBING

At tastings, you might feel pressure to join a wine club. Before you dismiss the idea, there are some benefits to consider. Joining a wine club affords you the chance to continue learning about wine, and also ensures that you'll develop a great inventory at home. Most wine clubs work by sending you three or four shipments a year. You can usually specify if you'd like to receive reds or whites or both, but you may end up with a few varietals that don't tickle your taste buds. Fees for wine clubs can range from $50 to $150 per shipment (and the shipping fees are generally included).

Some of the benefits of receiving wine club shipments are that you'll often get wines that are yet to be released to the public or special reserve wines that are not available anywhere else. Plus, most wine club members receive 10 to 20 percent discounts on purchases in addition to free tastings. There is rarely a cost to join a wine club and you can quit at any time.

Receiving great wine on a regular basis can be convenient, especially if you entertain often or are in the habit of enjoying a bottle at dinner. If you do join a club, you may want to purchase a wine refrigerator in which to store your collection. These can range from small, 12-bottle fridges, which cost around $150, to more elaborate 50-bottle thermo-electric contraptions with all kinds of bells and whistles. When it comes to storing wine, finding the right temperature is actually less important than maintaining consistency with that temperature. Wine holds up best when there are no fluctuations in temperature, humidity and darkness.

VINTAGE CORKS

## HOW TO READ A LABEL

Why look at the label? First of all, you should see it to make sure it's the wine you ordered (if you're in a restaurant). It can also tell you quite a bit about what you're drinking. Once you break it down into several digestible components, you'll be skimming labels like the titles on Netflix.

Here are the basics to look for:

### 1. Winemaker or Winery
This is the name of the company or vintner who makes the wine.

### 2. Appellation
The country or region where the grapes hail from. This can be as broad as "California," or as specific as "Santa Ynez Valley." An appellation may be as large as an entire region or as small as a few acres.

### 3. Vintage
This indicates which year the grapes are harvested. You might think it's the year in which the bottle is produced, but sometimes the wine isn't made for years after the harvest. However, most wine laws require that 85 percent of the wine be harvested in the year of its vintage.

### 4. Varietal
This connotes the specific kind of grapes from which the wine is made. Examples are chardonnay, syrah or cabernet sauvignon. If the wine is a blend of grapes, you might see a special name in place of the variety and then a breakdown of percentages. For instance, the variety may read "cuvée le bec" and underneath you will see "grenache 50 percent, syrah 28 percent, mourvedre 15 percent, counoise 7 percent."

### 5. Estate Bottling and Winery Information
If the wine is estate-bottled, it will say so underneath the vintage or varietal. Many wineries grow or purchase grapes offsite, so when they do grow and harvest the grapes in their own vineyards, they label them as such. You should also be able to find more winery information and an address of the vineyard on the back label of the bottle.

### 6. Required Information
Wines produced or imported to the U.S. require the typical government warning asking consumers to take health and safety precautions. You will also

# WINE UNFILTERED

find a disclaimer saying that the bottle contains sulfites (which may cause allergies) and sometimes an alcohol percentage will be disclosed.

## 7. Optional Information
Some vineyards will provide a history or blurb about their winery on the back of the bottle. Or, if it is a specially produced bottle, you may find more information about the winemaking process or find food-pairing suggestions.

# WINE VOCABULARY

Oenophiles have their own vino vernacular. Some phrases are more obvious than others, but the list below will acquaint you with some of the more commonly used terms. However, while there are dozens of designated ways to talk about wine, feel free to think about and describe it in the way that makes the most sense to you.

**Acidic** – tart or sour. Younger wines are usually more acidic than older ones.

**Aroma** – the portion of the fragrance that is derived specifically from the grape.

**Balance** – a wine whose portions of acidity, tannins and alcohol do not mask each other.

**Big** – a wine with a lot of flavor or alcohol.

**Bitter** – one of the basic taste elements. Tannins can make a wine particularly bitter.

**Bouquet** – the overall smell encompassing the grape from the fermentation process and the aging.

**Brilliant** – perfectly clear in appearance and usually an indicator of higher acidity.

**Buttery** – often used to describe chardonnay aged in oak.

**Clean** – having no bad odors or tastes.

**Clone** – a vine produced to better adapt to climate or geological conditions.

**Cloudy** – an opaque appearance found in wines that are intentionally unfiltered.

**Complex** – used to describe a wine whose many elements are distinguishable, or whose flavor changes sip to sip.

**Corked** – when a wine smells of cork, an indication that a wine has gone bad.

# WINE VOCABULARY

**Dry –** said of a wine that does not have an apparent sweetness.

**Earthy –** used to describe a wine that has a rich, loamy essence.

**Fermentation –** the process that turns grapes into wine, specifically the metabolization of the sugars by the yeast into alcohol.

**Finish –** the impression or flavors that linger after you have swallowed.

**Flat –** describes a wine that is not acidic.

**Flowery –** refers to a wine with a floral fragrance.

**Fruity –** refers to a wine with a fruit-based fragrance.

**Full –** akin to a "big" wine.

**Harvest –** the picking of the grapes. The first step of wine production.

**Hybrid –** grape varieties created in a lab that involve more than one variety.

**Late Harvest –** this indicates that grapes were left on the vine to ripen longer than usual.

**Legs –** the rivulets that run down the glass when the wine is swirled.

**Light –** a wine that offers more subtle flavors, or a lower alcohol content.

**Mellow –** used to describe a wine that is soft, smooth and lightly sweet.

**Nose –** refers to the bouquet or aroma.

**Oaky –** used to describe the flavor of wine that has been aged in oak barrels.

**Pressing –** the process in which the juice is squeezed from the grape, separating it from its skin.

**Tannin –** a bitter tasting material created in the winemaking process that helps preserve the wine.

**Terroir –** the French word for "soil" but can also refer to the climate, weather conditions and land in which the grapes were grown.

**Varietal –** the kind of grape from which the wine is made.

**Vintage –** the year the grape was harvested.

**Wine –** a way of life.

# INDEX

## Chapter 1: Napa Valley
Artesa Vineyard and Winery *(Napa, CA)*, 31
Auberge du Soleil *(Rutherford, CA)*, 28
Auberge du Soleil Restaurant *(Rutherford, CA)*, 28
Auberge du Soleil Spa *(Rutherford, CA)*, 29
The Bathhouse *(Calistoga, CA)*, 18
Beringer Vineyards *(St. Helena, CA)*, 19
Bouchaine Vineyards *(Napa, CA)*, 32
Bouchon *(Yountville, CA)*, 30
Calistoga Inn Restaurant and Brewery *(Calistoga, CA)*, 15
Calistoga Ranch *(Calistoga, CA)*, 17
The Carneros Inn *(Napa, CA)*, 34
Castello di Amorosa *(St. Helena, CA)*, 37
Ca'toga Galleria d'Arte *(Calistoga, CA)*, 18
Chamber Music Festival *(Napa Valley, CA)*, 39
Charbay Winery & Distillery *(St. Helena, CA)*, 19
Cliff Lede Vineyards *(Yountville, CA)*, 29
COPIA *(Napa, CA)*, 32
Culinary Institute of America at Greystone *(St. Helena, CA)*, 19
Darioush *(Napa, CA)*, 33
Dean and Deluca *(St. Helena, CA)*, 23
Domaine Carneros *(Napa, CA)*, 33
Domaine Chandon *(Yountville, CA)*, 30
Downtown Napa *(Napa, CA)*, 36
The French Laundry *(Yountville, CA)*, 31
Hartwell Vineyards *(Napa, CA)*, 37
Hurd Beeswax Candles *(Calistoga, CA)*, 18
The Inn at Southbridge *(St. Helena, CA)*, 21
Kelham Vineyards *(St. Helena, CA)*, 19
Kuleto Estate Vineyards *(St. Helena, CA)*, 20
Madrigal Vineyards *(Calistoga, CA)*, 15
Main Element *(Calistoga, CA)*, 19
Martini House *(St. Helena, CA)*, 21
Meadowood Napa Valley *(St. Helena, CA)*, 21
Merryvale Vineyards *(St. Helena, CA)*, 20
The Model Bakery *(St. Helena, CA)*, 23
Napa Soap Company *(St. Helena, CA)*, 24
Napa Valley Mustard Festival *(Napa Valley, CA)*, 39
Napa Valley Opera House *(Napa, CA)*, 36
Napa Valley Wine Train *(Napa, CA)*, 35
Oakville Grocery *(Oakville, CA)*, 35
Olivier Napa Valley *(St. Helena, CA)*, 24
Oxbow Public Market *(Napa, CA)*, 36
Patz and Hall *(Napa, CA)*, 33
Peju Province Winery *(Rutherford, CA)*, 26
Quixote Winery *(Napa, CA)*, 37
Redd *(Yountville, CA)*, 31
Regusci Winery *(Napa, CA)*, 33
The Restaurant at Meadowood *(St. Helena, CA)*, 22
Robert Sinskey Vineyards *(Napa, CA)*, 37
Round Pond Olive Mill *(Rutherford, CA)*, 27
Rubicon Estate *(Rutherford, CA)*, 26
St. Clement Vineyards *(St. Helena, CA)*, 20
St. Supéry Vineyards and Winery *(Rutherford, CA)*, 27
Schramsberg Vineyards *(Calistoga, CA)*, 16
Silver Oak Winery *(Napa, CA)*, 34
Solage Calistoga *(Calistoga, CA)*, 17
The Spa at The Carneros Inn *(Napa, CA)*, 35
The Spa at Meadowood *(St. Helena, CA)*, 24
Staglin Family Vineyard *(Rutherford, CA)*, 27
Sterling Vineyards *(Calistoga, CA)*, 16
Summer Music Festival at Robert Mondavi Winery *(Oakville, CA)*, 39
Taylor's Automatic Refresher *(St. Helena, CA)*, 23
Terra *(St. Helena, CA)*, 22
Ubuntu *(Napa, CA)*, 35
Vintage Inn *(Yountville, CA)*, 30
Wappo Bar and Bistro *(Calistoga, CA)*, 18
Wine Country Film Festival *(Napa Valley, CA)*, 39
Woodhouse Chocolate *(St. Helena, CA)*, 24
Yountville Festival of Lights *(Yountville, CA)*, 39

## Chapter 2: Sonoma Valley
14feet. *(Healdsburg, CA)*, 50
Bartholomew Park Winery *(Sonoma, CA)*, 43
Bella Vineyards and Wine Caves *(Healdsburg, CA)*, 48
Buena Vista Carneros Historic Tasting Room *(Sonoma, CA)*, 43
Carneros Bistro & Wine Bar *(Sonoma, CA)*, 45
Cyrus *(Healdsburg, CA)*, 49
Della Santina's *(Sonoma, CA)*, 46
Dry Creek Kitchen *(Healdsburg, CA)*, 50
El Dorado Hotel *(Sonoma, CA)*, 44
El Dorado Kitchen *(Sonoma, CA)*, 46
The Fairmont Sonoma Mission Inn & Spa *(Sonoma, CA)*, 44
The Girl and the Fig *(Sonoma, CA)*, 46
Gloria Ferrer Caves and Vineyards *(Sonoma, CA)*, 44
Harmony Lounge at the Ledson Hotel *(Sonoma, CA)*, 47
Hotel Healdsburg *(Healdsburg, CA)*, 48
Lambert Bridge Winery *(Healdsburg, CA)*, 48
Les Mars Hotel *(Healdsburg, CA)*, 49
Lime Stone *(Healdsburg, CA)*, 51
MacArthur Place *(Sonoma, CA)*, 45
Myra Hoefer Design *(Healdsburg, CA)*, 51
Preston of Dry Creek *(Healdsburg, CA)*, 48
Quivira Vineyards *(Healdsburg, CA)*, 48
Ravenswood *(Sonoma, CA)*, 44
San Francisco Solano, *(Sonoma, CA)*, 40
Scopa *(Healdsburg, CA)*, 50
Tiddle E. Winks *(Sonoma, CA)*, 47
The Vasquez House Library and Tea Room *(Sonoma, CA)*, 47
Vella Cheese Company *(Sonoma, CA)*, 47

## Chapter 3: Central Coast
Alma Rosa Winery *(Buellton, CA)*, 66
Aubergine *(Carmel-by-the-Sea, CA)*, 63
Babcock Winery *(Lompoc, CA)*, 66
Bacara Resort & Spa *(Santa Barbara, CA)*, 68, 71
Baja Cantina Grill and Filling Station *(Carmel, CA)*, 61
Bernardus Lodge *(Carmel Valley, CA)*, 59
Bernardus Winery *(Carmel Valley, CA)*, 55
Boëté Winery *(Carmel Valley, CA)*, 55
Bouchee *(Carmel-by-the-Sea, CA)*, 63
Bouchon *(Santa Barbara, CA)*, 70
Café Rustica *(Carmel Valley, CA)*, 61
Canary Hotel *(Santa Barbara, CA)*, 69
Chateau Julien Winery *(Carmel, CA)*, 56
The Cheese Shop *(Carmel-by-the-Sea, CA)*, 63

# INDEX

Club Jalapeño *(Carmel-by-the-Sea, CA)*, 64
The Covey *(Carmel, CA)*, 62
Cypress Inn *(Carmel, CA)*, 60
D'Angelo Bread *(Santa Barbara, CA)*, 71
Downey's *(Santa Barbara, CA)*, 70
Earthbound Farms *(Carmel, CA)*, 62
East Beach *(Santa Barbara, CA)*, 72
El Paseo de Santa Barbara *(Santa Barbara, CA)*, 73
Firestone Vineyard *(Los Olivos, CA)*, 67
Foley Estates Vineyard & Winery *(Lompoc, CA)*, 67
Four Seasons Resort The Biltmore Santa Barbara *(Santa Barbara, CA)*, 68
Foxen Vineyards *(Santa Maria, CA)*, 67
Georis Winery *(Carmel Valley, CA)*, 56
Grape Express *(Monterey, CA)*, 59
Heller Estate *(Carmel Valley, CA)*, 57
Highlands Inn, A Hyatt Hotel *(Carmel, CA)*, 60
Hungry Cat *(Santa Barbara, CA)*, 71
Joullian Vineyards *(Carmel Valley, CA)*, 57
La Super-Rica Taqueria *(Santa Barbara, CA)*, 71
L'Auberge *(Carmel-by-the-Sea, CA)*, 61
Los Olivos Wine Merchant & Café *(Los Olivos, CA)*, 67
Market Forays with Laurence Hauben *(Santa Barbara, CA)*, 73
Marinus *(Carmel Valley, CA)*, 62
Melville Vineyards & Winery *(Lompoc, CA)*, 68
Miró *(Santa Barbara, CA)*, 70
Mission Ranch *(Carmel, CA)*, 61
Mission Santa Barbara *(Santa Barbara, CA)*, 73
Morgan Winery *(Carmel, CA)*, 57
Olio e Limone *(Santa Barbara, CA)*, 71
Panino *(Solvang, CA)*, 67
Parsonage *(Carmel Valle, CA)*, 58
Quail Lodge Resort and Golf Club *(Carmel, CA)*, 60
San Ysidro Ranch, A Rosewood Resort *(Montecito, CA)*, 69
Santa Barbara Shellfish Company *(Santa Barbara, CA)*, 71
The Spa at Bernardus Lodge *(Carmel Valley, CA)*, 64
Spa at Four Seasons Resort The Biltmore Santa Barbara *(Santa Barbara, CA)*, 72
Stearns Wharf and Ty Warner Sea Center *(Santa Barbara, CA)*, 73
Talbott Vineyards *(Carmel Valley, CA)*, 58
The Wine Trolley *(Monterey, CA)*, 59

## Chapter 4: Oregon Wine Country
The Ace Hotel *(Portland, OR)*, 85
Adelsheim Vineyard *(Newberg, OR)*, 77
Andina *(Portland, OR)*, 86
Argyle Winery *(Dundee, OR)*, 77
Avalon Hotel *(Portland, OR)*, 83
Avalon Spa *(Portland, OR)*, 89
The Bee and Thistle *(Portland, OR)*, 89
Bistro Maison *(McMinnville, OR)*, 84
Black Walnut Inn *(Dundee, OR)*, 84
Bluehour *(Portland, OR)*, 86
Brick House Vineyards *(Newberg, OR)*, 77
Cheeky B *(Portland, OR)*, 89
Cristom Vineyards *(Salem, OR)*, 84
Domaine Drouhin Oregon *(Dayton, OR)*, 78
Domaine Serene *(Dayton, OR)*, 78
Doug Fir *(Portland, OR)*, 90
Dundee Bistro & Wine Bar *(Dundee, OR)*, 84
Eco Tours of Oregon *(Portland, OR)*, 81
Entourage International Limousines *(Portland, OR)*, 81
Executive Limousine Company *(Portland, OR)*, 81
The Eyrie Vineyards *(McMinnville, OR)*, 79
The Four Graces Vineyards *(Dundee, OR)*, 79
Genoa *(Portland, OR)*, 86
Grape Escape Winery Tour *(Portland, OR)*, 81
Heathman Hotel *(Portland, OR)*, 83
Hotel deLuxe *(Portland, OR)*, 85
Ken's Artisan Bakery *(Portland, OR)*, 82
Le Pigeon *(Portland, OR)*, 87
Lizard Lounge *(Portland, OR)*, 89
Meriwether's *(Portland, OR)*, 82
My Chauffeur Wine Tours *(Portland, OR)*, 81
Oregon Wine Tours *(Portland, OR)*, 81
Paley's Place *(Portland, OR)*, 88
Penner-Ash Wine Cellars *(Newberg, OR)*, 80
Pok Pok *(Portland, OR)*, 88
Ponzi Vineyards *(Beaverton, OR)*, 80
Powell's City of Books *(Portland, OR)*, 89
Premiere Tours *(Portland, OR)*, 81
Sokol Blosser *(Portland, OR)*, 80
St. Honoré Boulangerie *(Portland, OR)*, 87
St. Innocent *(Salem, OR)*, 86
Stumptown Coffee Roasters *(Portland, OR)*, 88
Willakenzie Estate *(Yamhill, OR)*, 82
Willamette Tours *(Portland, OR)*, 81

## Chapter 5: Washington Wine Country
The 5th Avenue Theatre *(Seattle, WA)*, 103
ACT Theatre *(Seattle, WA)*, 103
Alderwood Mall *(Lynnwood, WA)*, 102
Betz Family Winery *(Redmond, WA)*, 93
Bon Vivant Wine Tours *(Woodinville, WA)*, 97
Brian Carter Cellars *(Woodinville, WA)*, 93
Bumbershoot *(Seattle, WA)*, 104
Café Flora *(Seattle, WA)*, 99
Century Ballroom *(Seattle, WA)*, 103
Chateau Ste. Michelle *(Woodinville, WA)*, 93
Columbia Winery *(Woodinville, WA)*, 95
Dimitriou's Jazz Alley *(Seattle, WA)*, 103
Downtown Shopping District *(Seattle, WA)*, 102
Etta's Seafood *(Seattle, WA)*, 99
The Fairmont Olympic Hotel *(Seattle, WA)*, 96
Fremont Oktoberfest *(Seattle, WA)*, 104
The Georgian *(Seattle, WA)*, 100
The Herbfarm *(Woodinville, WA)*, 100
Hotel Monaco *(Seattle, WA)*, 97
Hotel Vintage Park *(Seattle, WA)*, 98
Inn at the Market *(Seattle, WA)*, 98
Januik Winery *(Woodinville, WA)*, 95
Lampreia Restaurant *(Seattle, WA)*, 100
Mayflower Park Hotel *(Seattle, WA)*, 98
Napolitano Day Sap Salon *(Seattle, WA)*, 101
Page Cellars *(Woodinville, WA)*, 96
Passport to Woodinville *(Woodinville, WA)*, 105
Purple Café and Wine Bar *(Woodinville, WA)*, 101
Saint Nicholas Day *(Woodinville, WA)*, 105
Seattle Art Museum *(Seattle, WA)*, 103
Silver Lake Winery *(Woodinville, WA)*, 96
Sur La Table *(Seattle, WA)*, 102
University Village Shopping *(Seattle, WA)*, 102
Willows Lodge *(Woodinville, WA)*, 99
Winery Bus *(Woodinville, WA)*, 97

# INDEX

**Chapter 6: Canada's Okanagan Valley**
Absolute Spa at the Century *(Vancouver, BC)*, 117
Arts Club Theatre Company *(Vancouver, BC)*, 119
Ballet British Columbia *(Vancouver, BC)*, 119
Bishop's *(Vancouver, BC)*, 115
Bliss Bakery *(Peachland, BC)*, 117
Bouchons *(Kelowna, BC)*, 117
British Columbia Wine Information Centre *(Penticton, BC)*, 118
Burrowing Owl Estate Winery *(Oliver, BC)*, 109
CedarCreek Estate Winery *(Kelowna, BC)*, 109
Coast Capri Hotel *(Kelowna, BC)*, 114
The Cove Lakeside Resort *(Westbank, BC)*, 115
Dirty Laundry Vineyard *(Summerland, BC)*, 110
Festival of the Grape *(Oliver, BC)*, 120
Four Seasons Hotel Vancouver *(Vancouver, BC)*, 114
Heritage District, Vancouver *(Vancouver, BC)*, 118
Inniskillin Okanagan Vineyards *(Oliver, BC)*, 110
Kelowna Art Gallery *(Kelowna, BC)*, 119
La Belle Auberge *(Ladner, BC)*, 116
Lake City Casinos *(Kelowna, BC)*, 120
Lumière *(Vancouver, BC)*, 116
Mission Hill Family Estate *(Westbank, BC)*, 111
Monashee Adventure Tours *(Kelowna, BC)*, 113
Nk'Mip Cellars *(Osoyoos, BC)*, 111
Okanagan Wine Country Tours *(Kelowna, BC)*, 113
Okanagan Wine Festivals *(Kelowna, BC)*, 121
Perfect Health Spa *(Vancouver, BC)*, 118
Quails' Gate *(Kelowna, BC)*, 111
Robson Street *(Vancouver, BC)*, 119
South Granville *(Vancouver, BC)*, 119
Sumac Ridge Estate Winery *(Summerland, BC)*, 112
Summerhill Pyramid Winery *(Kelowna, BC)*, 112
Summerland Waterfront Resort *(Summerland, BC)*, 115
The Sutton Place Hotel *(Vancouver, BC)*, 115
TRK Helicopter Charters (Langley, BC), 113
Vancouver Symphony Orchestra *(Vancouver, BC)*, 120
The Vanilla Pod Restaurant *(Summerland, BC)*, 117
West *(Vancouver, BC)*, 116

**Chapter 7: Long Island Wine Country**
The Baker House 1650 *(East Hampton, NY)*, 132
Bridgehampton Candy Kitchen *(Bridgehampton, NY)*, 132
Castello di Borghese *(Cutchogue, NY)*, 125
Channing Daughters Winery *(Bridgehampton, NY)*, 131
The Coffey House Bed and Breakfast *(East Marion, NY)*, 128
Collette Consignment *(Southampton, NY)*, 133
Della Femina *(East Hampton, NY)*, 132
The Frisky Oyster *(Greenport, NY)*, 129
Harborfront Inn at Greenport *(Greenport, NY)*, 129
Lieb Family Cellars *(Mattituck, NY)*, 127
Martha Clara Vineyards *(Riverhead, NY)*, 127
Osprey's Dominion Vineyards *(Peconic, NY)*, 128
Pindar Vineyards *(Peconic, NY)*, 128
The Seafood Barge *(Southold, NY)*, 130
Seatuck Cove House *(Eastport, NY)*, 129
The Surf Lodge *(Montauk, NY)*, 129
Verbena *(Greenport, NY)*, 130
The Village Cheese Shop *(Mattituck, NY)*, 131
Wölffer Estate Vineyard *(Sagaponack, NY)*, 131

**Chapter 8: Texas Hill Country**
Alamosa Wine Cellars *(Bend, TX)*, 137
The Antlers Hotel *(Kingsland, TX)*, 143
Austin Aloha Limousine *(Austin, TX)*, 141
Austin Museum of Art *(Austin, TX)*, 146
Austin Wine Festival *(Austin, TX)*, 140
Becker Vineyards (Stonewall, TX), 137
Bluffton Store *(Bluffton, TX)*, 139
Chocolate Festival *(Austin, TX)*, 140
The Driskill *(Austin, TX)*, 141
Driskill Grill *(Austin, TX)*, 143
Fall Creek Vineyards *(Tow, TX)*, 138
Flat Creek Estate *(Marble Falls, TX)*, 138
Fonda San Miguel *(Austin, TX)*, 143
Four Seasons Hotel Austin *(Austin, TX)*, 142
Fredericksburg Wine and Food Fest *(Fredericksburg, TX)*, 140
Horseshoe Bay Resort Marriott *(Horseshoe Bay, TX)*, 143
Hotel San José *(Austin, TX)*, 142
Hudson's on the Bend *(Austin, TX)*, 144
Lady Bird Johnson Wildflower Center *(Austin, TX)*, 146
LakeHouse Spa at Lake Austin Spa Resort *(Austin, TX)*, 145
Mandola Estate Winery *(Driftwood, TX)*, 140
The Mansion at Judges' Hill *(Austin, TX)*, 142
New World Wine and Food Festival *(San Antonio, TX)*, 140
Sixth Street *(Austin, TX)*, 146
South Congress Avenue Shopping *(Austin, TX)*, 146
South Congress Café *(Austin, TX)*, 144
The Spa at Four Seasons Austin *(Austin, TX)*, 145
Texas Hill Country Wine and Food Festival *(Austin, TX)*, 140
Texas Wine Tours *(Fredericksburg, TX)*, 141
Torre di Pietra Winery *(Fredericksburg, TX)*, 139
Trattoria Lisina *(Driftwood, TX)*, 145
Trio *(Austin, TX)*, 144
Wildseed Farms *(Fredericksburg, TX)*, 140
Wine Tating Tours of Horseshoe Bay *(Horseshoe Bay, TX)*, 141

**Chapter 9: Virginia Monticello Wine Trail**
1804 Inn *(Barboursville, VA)*, 155
Afton Mountain *(Afton, VA)*, 149
And George *(Charlottesville, VA)*, 159
Barboursville Vineyards *(Barboursville, VA)*, 149
Basic Necessities *(Nellysford, VA)*, 160
Bavarian Chef *(Shelby, VA)*, 158
Boar's Head Inn *(Charlottesville, VA)*, 154
C&O *(Charlottesville, VA)*, 157
Fermentation Trap *(Barboursville, VA)*, 160
First Colony Winery *(Charlottesville, VA)*, 151

# ART CREDITS

Fountain Room at the Mark Addy *(Nellysford, VA)*, 158
Fossett's at Keswick Hall *(Keswick, VA)*, 157
Inn at Little Washington *(Washington, VA)*, 154, 157
Inn at Monticello *(Charlottesville, VA)*, 156
Ivy Inn *(Charlottesville, VA)*, 157
Jefferson Vineyards *(Charlottesville, VA)*, 151
Keswick Hall *(Keswick, VA)*, 154
Keswick Vineyards *(Keswick, VA)*, 152
L'Etoile *(Charlottesville, VA)*, 159
The Mark Addy *(Nellysford, VA)*, 156
Monticello Museum Shop *(Charlottesville, VA)*, 161
The Odd Chest *(Gordonsville, VA)*, 161
Old Mill Room at the Boars Head Inn *(Charlottesville, VA)*, 158
Palladio Restaurant at Barboursville *(Barboursville, VA)*, 159
Prince Michel *(Leon, VA)*, 152
Rockfish Gap Country Store *(Afton, VA)*, 161
Veritas Winery *(Afton, VA)*, 153
Wintergreen Resort *(Winterreen, VA)*, 155
Wintergreen Winery *(Nellysford, VA)*, 153
The White Pig *(Schuyler, VA)*, 156

## ART CREDITS

**Illustrations**
All maps: ©Ken Gross for Rustbelt Cartography

**Introduction**
Quails' Gate Vineyard in the Okanagan: Brian Sprout/Okanagan Wine Festivals
Coastal Vineyards: Istock
Wine glass and book: Courtesy of Bernardus Lodge and Winery
Oregon Vineyards: Domaine Serene

**Chapter 1: Napa Valley**
Scenic View: Auberge du Soleil
Summer Gardens: The Vintage Inn
Gustroom: The Vintage Inn
Veranda: Copyright Matthew Millman/Solage Calistoga
Scenic Plunge Pool: Auberge du Soleil
View of the Vineyards: Solage Calistoga
Owner's Lodge: Calistoga Ranch
Wine Cave: Calistoga Ranch
Winery: Schramsberg Vineyards
Guestroom: Solage Calistoga
Front Entrance: Wappo Bar and Bistro
Outdoor Tables: Kuleto Estate Winery
Dalo Lane Vineyards: Beringer Vineyards
Rhine House: Beringer Vineyards
Balcony: Meadowood Napa Valley
Dining: Meadowood Napa Valley
St Clement Winery: St Clement Winery
Vineyards: Kuleto Estate Vineyard
Fireplace Dining: Martini House
Diffuser: Napa Soap Company
Spa Room: Auberge du Soleil
Tasting: Herta Peju/Peju Province Winery
Winery: Herta Peju/Peju Province Winery
Winery Terrace: Cleff Lede Vineyards
Vineyards: Rocco Ceselin/Peju Province Winery
Guestroom: Auberge du Soleil
Outdoor Restaurant: Auberge du Soleil
Inn and Gardens: The Vintage Inn
The French Laundry: The French Laundry
Guestroom: Mark Hundley/Carneros Inn
Napa: Brent Miller/www.winecountry.com
Ubuntu: Scott Nugent/designthis.com
Hand Made Soaps: Napa Soap Company
Napa Valley Wine Train: Trenton McManus
Napa Valley Opera House: David Wakely
Napa Valley Wine Train: Robert Holmes/California Tourism 1997
Oxbow Public Market: Frankie Frankeny
Napa: Brent Miller/www.winecountry.com

**Chapter 2: Sonoma Valley**
Firepit Patio: The Lodge at Sonoma
Salad: The Fairmont Sonoma Mission Inn
Spa: The Fairmont Sonoma Mission Inn
Pool at Night: The Lodge at Sonoma
Vineyard in Light: Laurence Bartone/Glorier Ferrer Caves and Vineyards
Spa: The Fairmont Sonoma Mission Inn
Restaurant Sign: El Dorado Kitchen
Lavender: Istock
Restaurant: The Lodge at Sonoma
Sonoma Coastline: Robert Janover/www.sonomacounty.com
Tasting Room: Patz and Hall
Balloons over Sonoma: Up and Away Ballooning/www.sonomacounty.com
Downtown Healdsburg: Bradley J. Gillette
Pool: Cesar Rubio/Hotel Healdsburg
Suite: Cesar Rubio/Hotel Healdsburg
Wine Cave: Lily Hill/Bella Vineyards and Wine Caves
Exterior: Cesar Rubio/Hotel Healdsburg
Dining: Cesar Rubio/Dry Creek Kitchen
Lime Stone : Lime Stone Healdsburg

**Chapter 3: Central Coast**
Chateau: Chateau Julien Wine Estate
Sunflowers: Earthbound Farm
Salad: Aaron Cook/The Hungry Cat
Alma Rosa Tasting Room: Robert Szerwo/Alma Rosa Winery and Vineyard
Fire Pit: Peter Vitale/Four Seasons Biltmore Santa Barbara
Morgan Winery Vineyards: Morgan Winery
Pathway: Chateau Julien Wine Estate
Strawberry's: Melissa Fargo/Santa Barbara CVB
Great Hall: Chateau Julien Wine Estate
Wine Tasting: Chateau Julien Wine Estate
Vineyard: Chateau Julien Wine Estate
Talbott Vineyards: Talbott Vineyards
Lobby at Bernardus Lodge: Courtesy of Bernardus Lodge and Winery
Mission Ranch: Carmel California
Earthboud Farm Stand: Earthbound Farm
Mission Ranch: Kerrick James/Monterey County CVB
The Covey: Quail Lodge Resort
Earthbound Farm: Earthbound Farm
Marinus Restaurant Salad: Courtesy of Bernardus Lodge and Winery
Hydrotherapy Tub: Courtesy of Bernardus Lodge and Winery
Rooftops: Santa Barbara CVB
Alma Rosa Vineyards: Deborah Denker/Alma Rosa Winery and Vineyard
Guest Room at San Ysidro Ranch: San Ysidro Ranch/Rosewood Resorts
Spa at Night: Bacara Resort and Spa
The Four Seasons: Barbara Kraft/The Four Seasons Biltmore Santa Barbara
Four Poster: Canary Hotel Santa Barbara
Ranch at Dusk: San Ysidro Ranch/Rosewood Resorts
Bacara Resort: Bacara Resort and Spa
Dining: Aaron Cook/The Hungry Cat
Santa Barbara Mission Courtyard: Melissa Fargo/ Santa Barbara CVB

# ART CREDITS

### Chapter 4: Oregon Wine Country
St Honore: Basil Childers/St Honore
Vineyard: Kevin Bell/Domaine Drouhin
Dining at Andina: Basil Childers/Andina
Pastry Hearts: Basil Childers/St Honore
Oregon Wine Country: Istock
Winery: Kevin Bell/Domaine Drouhin
Sokol Blosser: Doreen L.Wynja/Sokol Blosser Winery
Portland Oregon: Travel Portland
Avalon Hotel Suite: Avalon Hotel and Spa
Portland Oregon: Travel Portland
Tea: Basil Childers/Heathman Restaurant
Sokol Blosser: Doreen L. Wynja/Sokol Blosser Winery
Winery: Kevin Bell/Domaine Drouhin
Sokol Blosser: Doreen L. Wynja/Sokol Blosser Winery
Lobby: The Heathman Hotel
Lobby at Hotel DeLuxe: Hotel DeLuxe
Andina: Basil Childers/Andina
Avalon Exterior: Avalon Hotel and Spa
King Bedroom: Hotel DeLuxe
The Ace Hotel: Lauren Coleman
Andina: Basil Childers/Andina
River View: Avalon Hotel and Spa
Portland Skyline: Travel Portland

### Chapter 5: Washington Wine Country
Out door Tasting: Brian Carter Cellars
Bedroom Suite: Fairmont Olympic Hotel
Red Vines: Istock
Suite: John Valls/Hotel Vintage Park
Chapel in the Vineyards: Columbia Winery
Exterior Gardens: Fairmont Olympic Hotel
Tasting Patio: Silver Lake Winery
Columbia Winery: Columbia Winery
Woodinville Vineyards: Istock
Salad: The Georgian Restaurant
Lobby: David Phelps/Hotel Monaco
Vines: Silver Lake Winery
Bedroom: John Valls/Hotel Vintage Park
Dining: Kate Baldwin/Purple Restaurant
Gallery: R Barnes/Seattle Art Museum
Fritter: Ilya Moshenskiy/Café Flora
Dining Room: The Georgian Restaurant
Shopping Cart: Sur La Table Seattle
Jazz: Dimitrou's Jazz Alley
Seattle Waterfront: Tim Thompson/Seattle Convention and Visitors Bureau
Giant Barrel: Fremont Oktoberfest

### Chapter 6: Canada's Okanagain Valley
Vineyards: Brian Sprout/Quails' Gate Vineyards/Okanagan Wine Festivals
Cedar Creek Ranch: Brian Sprout/Cedar Creek Winery
Bottles: Cedar Creek Estate Winery
Spirit Ridge: Courtesy of Spirit Ridge
Sumac Ridge Vineyards: Brian Sprout/Sumac Ridge Estate Winery
Vineyards: Brian Sprout/Inniskillen Winery
Patio View: Quails' Gate Winery
Winery: Burrowing Owl Estate Winery
Vineyards: Brian Sprout/Quails' Gate Winery
Patio: Courtesy of Nk'Mip Cellars
Wine Bottle: Sumac Ridge Estate Winery
Vineyard: Brian Sprout/Cedar Creek Estate Winery
Wine Barrels: Inniskillen Winery
Guest Room: Four Seasons Vancouver
Pool: Coast Capri Hotels and Resorts
Dining at the Four Seasons: John Sherlock/The Four Seasons Vancouver
Fruit Pavlova: Lumiere Restaurant
West Restaurant: West Vancouver
Dining Tables: Lumiere Restaurant
Spa: Absolute Spa at the Century
Treatment Room: Perfect Health Spa
Gallery: Colin Jewall/Kelowna Art Gallery

### Chapter 7: Long Island Wine Country
Long Island Wine Country: Istock
Sound: Long Island Wine Council
Indoor Pool: The Baker House 1650
Winery: Channing Daughters Winery
Beach: www.discoverlongisland.com
Long Island Vineyards: Istock
Fountain: Wolffer Estate Vineyards
Wine Country: Long Island Wine Council
Steak and Fries: Heike Sauerland
Wine Barrels: Castello Di Borghese
Vineyards: Channing Daughters Winery
Merlot: Wolffer Estate Vineyards
Tasting Rooms: Wolffer Estate Vineyards
House and Gardens: The Coffey House
Cottage Exterior: The Baker House 1650
Seafood Barge: Heike Sauerland
Beach: www.discoverlong island.com
Boats: Long Island Wine Council
Vineyards: Wolffer Estate Vineyards

### Chapter 8: Texas Hill Country
Mexican Entre: Fonda San Miguel
Trio: Cesar Rubio/Four Seasons Austin
Lake House Spa: Lake Austin Spa Resort
Tasting: Marc Bennet/Grape Creek Winery
Mist on the Lake: Lake Austin Spa Resort
Fields: Wildseed Farms/Fredericksburg CVB
Vines: Robert Anschutz/Flat Creek Estate
Wildseed Farms Barn: Wildseed Farms
Alamosa Winery: Alamosa Wine Cellars
Lobby: The Driskill Hotel
Mojitos: Fonda San Miguel
Peaches: Jim Fox/Fredericksburg CVB
Trio: Cesar Rubio/Four Seasons Austin
Foyer: The Mansion at Judges Hill
Spa: Kevin Syms/Four Seasons Austin
Entrance: The Mansion at Judges Hill
Trio: Stacy Sodolak/Four Seasons Austin
Waiting Area: Lake Austin Spa Resort
Dusk: Gary Kufner/Horseshoe Bay Resort
Shopping on South Congress Avenue
Austin: Peter Vitale/Four Seasons Austin

### Chapter 9: Virginia Monticello Wine Trail
Bedroom: Courtesy of Boar's Head Inn
Palladio Dining: Barboursville Vineyards
Sunset: The Mark Addy Inn
Floral Room: The Inn at Little Washington
Keswick Hall and Grounds: Sequoia/Orient Express Hotels
Vineyards: Barboursville Vineyards
Vineyards: Veritas Winery
Grapes: Keswick Hall/Orient Express Hotels
Night: Sequoia/Orient Express Hotels
Pool: Sequoia/Orient Express Hotels
Fountain: The Mark Addy Inn
Monticello: Roy Van Doorn/Monticello
Hunt Club: Courtesy of Boar's Head Inn
Veranda: Gordon Beall/The Inn at Little Washington
Fossetts: Sequoia/Orient Express Hotels
Virginian Vineyards: Keith Lanpher/VTC
Suite: Sequoia/Orient Express Hotels
Fossetts: Sequoia/Orient Express Hotels
Bistro: Courtesy of Boar's Head Inn
Sparkling Wine: Barboursville Vineyards
Flags: The Inn at Little Washington
Vineyards: Barboursville Vineyards

### Chapter 10: Wine Unfiltered
Red Wine Tasting; White Wine Against the Light; White Wine in Scenic Napa; Red, White, Rose; Swirling; Chilling: Istock
Patio View: Nk'Mip Cellars
Sparkling Blends: Schramsberg Vineyards